英 Make Me High 系列
語

英文寫作測驗：
句子合併 & 克漏式翻譯

Writing Test:

Sentence Combination & Guided Translation

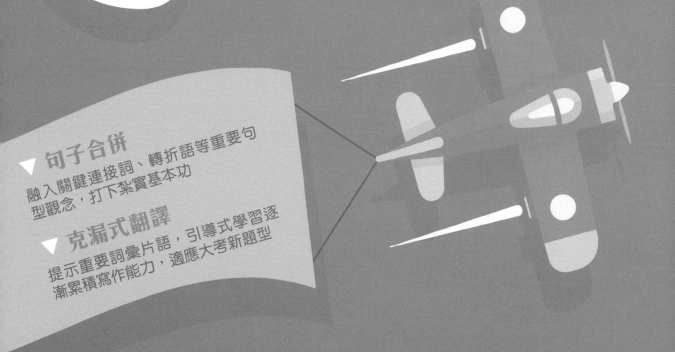

▼ **句子合併**

融入關鍵連接詞、轉折語等重要句型觀念，打下紮實基本功

▼ **克漏式翻譯**

提示重要詞彙片語，引導式學習逐漸累積寫作能力，適應大考新題型

國家圖書館出版品預行編目資料

Writing Test:Sentence Combination & Guided Translation 英文寫作測驗：句子合併&克漏式翻譯／王隆興編著.——初版十刷.——臺北市：三民，2021
面； 公分.——（英語Make Me High系列）

4712780666722 （平裝）
1. 英語 2. 問題集 3. 中等教育

524.38   98013780

Writing Test:Sentence Combination & Guided Translation
英文寫作測驗──句子合併&克漏式翻譯

編 著 者	王隆興
發 行 人	劉振強
出 版 者	三民書局股份有限公司
地 址	臺北市復興北路 386 號 (復北門市) 臺北市重慶南路一段 61 號 (重南門市)
電 話	(02)25006600
網 址	三民網路書店 https://www.sanmin.com.tw
出版日期	初版一刷 2009 年 8 月 初版十刷 2021 年 5 月
書籍編號	S808240
	4712780666722

三民書局

序

英語 Make Me High 系列的理想在於超越，在於創新。

這是時代的精神，也是我們出版的動力；

這是教育的目的，也是我們進步的執著。

針對英語的全球化與未來的升學趨勢，

我們設計了一系列適合普高、技高學生的英語學習書籍。

面對英語，不會徬徨不再迷惘，學習的心徹底沸騰，

心情好 High！

實戰模擬，掌握先機知己知彼，百戰不殆決勝未來，

分數更 High！

選擇優質的英語學習書籍，才能激發學習的強烈動機；

興趣盎然便不會畏懼艱難，自信心要自己大聲說出來。

本書如良師指引循循善誘，如益友相互鼓勵攜手成長。

展書輕閱，你將發現……

學習英語原來也可以這麼 High！

給讀者的話

　　將簡單的兩個句子用連接詞或轉折語 (transitional expressions) 合併，使其成為一個句意通順，並能涵蓋原本兩句句意的獨立句子，是訓練寫作的基礎方法之一。而克漏式翻譯除了測驗同學閱讀能力之外，更是精進寫作不可或缺的一環。這就是本書出版的目的。

　　本書專為訓練同學翻譯與作文而做。不論是學測或指考，翻譯加作文共計二十八分，比重不可謂不重。根據統計，大部份的考生，翻譯得分比例都低於作文。可見由於句意的限制，翻譯部份對考生而言較難下筆。本書特別針對考生弱點，設計克漏式翻譯，加強其閱讀與翻譯能力。其內容都是與考生日常生活貼近的題材，句型都不複雜，同學可以參考提示，多加演練。句子合併部分，都是最簡單的基本句型。希望藉由淺顯易懂的句意合併，建立同學信心，同時培養同學實力。相信經由本書所提供的訓練，同學能在學測或指考翻譯和作文部份獲得高分。

　　本書之所以能順利付梓，要感謝三民書局編輯部同仁對本書的精心規劃與編排，以及鉅細靡遺的校對。然而筆者才學疏淺，疏漏之處在所難免，望先進不吝指正。

王隆興
於臺北市立南港高中

 **Contents**

Abbreviations

Adj	Adjective 形容詞
Adj-er	形容詞的比較級
Adv	Adverb 副詞
Adv-er	副詞的比較級
Aux	Auxiliary 助動詞
N	Noun 名詞
O	Object 受詞
OC	Object Complement 受詞補語
Prep.	Preposition 介係詞
S	Subject 主詞
sb.	somebody 某人
sth.	something 某事
that-clause	that 所引導的子句
V	Verb 動詞（原形動詞）
V-ed	Past Tense 過去式
V-en	Past Participle 過去分詞
V-ing	Present Participle/ Gerund 現在分詞/ 動名詞
wh-	Wh 開頭的疑問詞 (What/ Why/ When/ Where/ How)

英文寫作測驗：句子合併&克漏式翻譯

Writing Test: Sentence Combination & Guided Translation

實力養成篇

Sentence Combination 句子合併

說明 請根據提示，將各題的兩個句子合併成一個語意通順、語法正確的英文句子。

1. although

George has failed in English tests for two times.

George still does not give up.

 _____

2. neither...nor...

I did not stay at home last Sunday.

I did not go picnicking with my friends last Sunday.

 _____

3. due to

The final soccer game was postponed.

There was a heavy storm.

 _____

due to/owing to/because of/as a result of + N 因為

4. since

Nancy started sleeping at three o'clock.

Nancy is still sleeping now.

 _____

since + 確切時間 / 過去時間副詞 / 過去式子句

5. if

I did not have enough money last year.

I could not buy a new car last year.

 _____

Guided Translation 克漏式翻譯

說明 下面一段短文中，有數處以中文呈現，請利用上下文線索及提示（如單字、片語等）將其譯成正確、通順、達意且前後連貫的英文。

1. 大部分的人偶而都會感到疲倦。 The best way to keep away from fatigue is to follow a healthy diet. 2. 適當的飲食是避免疲倦的最容易方法之一 since our bodies need fuel to carry out daily functions such as digestion, blood circulation, and waste removal. 3. 另外一個避免疲倦的方法就是規律的運動。 Most jobs are computer-based now, forcing us to sit still all day long. 4. 因此，很多人變胖 because they are not burning enough calories. 5. 運動，像慢跑、健走，游泳等等， builds muscle and reduces body fat.

> ❶ sometimes/once in a while/from time to time 偶而，有時候
>   tiredness/fatigue 疲倦
> ❸ exercise regularly 規律運動
> ❹ therefore/as a result 因此   gain weight/put on weight/become heavy 變胖
> ❺ and so on/etc. 等等

1. _____

2. _____

3. _____

4. _____

5. _____

Sentence Combination 句子合併

說明 請根據提示，將各題的兩個句子合併成一個語意通順、語法正確的英文句子。

1. where

I was born in Fongyuan.

I spent my childhood in Fongyuan.

➦ _____

2. not only...but also

Hillary rented a new apartment for her son.

Hillary bought a new car for her daughter.

➦ _____

3. than

Grace weighs 150 pounds.

Jean weighs 130 pounds.

➦ _____

4. as a result

Fred didn't study hard.

Fred flunked three subjects.

➦ _____

as a result/therefore 因此　flunk （成績）不及格、當掉

5. taken

The car is made in Germany.

The police took the car away.

➦ _____

Guided Translation 克漏式翻譯

說明　下面一段短文中，有數處以中文呈現，請利用上下文線索及提示（如單字、片語等）將其譯成正確、通順、達意且前後連貫的英文。

The High Speed Rail debuted in Taiwan in 2007. These fast trains are one of the few modern railroad systems around the world. Now the Taiwan High Speed Rail runs around 134 trains every day from Taipei to Kaohsiung. 1. 這些車廂區分為兩種等級。 You can choose a standard car or a business car. 2. 商務車廂比較舒適，但標準車廂比較便宜。 The High Speed Rail train has a very powerful engine and uses special train tracks, so 3. 這些列車製造的噪音和污染要比汽車來得少。 The High Speed Rail stations are clean and specially designed. 4. 這些車站需要有很長的月台 where passengers can get on this long train conveniently. 5. 下次何不試著搭高鐵看看？

---

❶ be divided into 區分　class 等級
❸ less + 單數不可數名詞
❹ platform 月台
❺ why not + V 何不⋯？　try + V-ing 試試看

---

1. _____

2. _____

3. _____

4. _____

5. _____

3

Sentence Combination 句子合併

說明 請根據提示，將各題的兩個句子合併成一個語意通順、語法正確的英文句子。

1. both

Johnny enjoys going to the movies.

Jimmy enjoys going to the movies.

↪ _____

2. that

Brian is going to tell us a touching story.

The touching story happened three years ago.

↪ _____

3. only to

Angelina arrived at the airport in time.

Angelina found that she did not have her passport with her.

↪ _____

only to V 卻…

4. who

Four people were saved from the burning house.

Jenny was one of them.

↪ _____

5. when

Brad will reach Taipei tonight.

I will invite Brad over to have dinner.

↪ _____

invite sb. over 邀請…做客

Guided Translation 克漏式翻譯

說明 下面一段短文中，有數處以中文呈現，請利用上下文線索及提示（如單字、片語等）將其譯成正確、通順、達意且前後連貫的英文。

The United States has spent a great deal of time and money on national defense and intelligence. 1. 美國人認為他們的國家是世上最強的，but the 911 terrorist attack shattered their dream. 2. 數以千計的生命就這樣失去了 and 3. 他們很震驚有人會用這種方式攻擊他們國家。 However, the terrorists believed they were performing the acts of justice. 4. 他們準備好為他們的信仰而死， and they were proud to sacrifice their lives for brave deed. 5. 很不幸地，恐怖份子成為世界潛在的敵人。

❶ the most powerful/strongest 最強的
❷ thousands of 數以千計
❸ be extremely shocked 極度震驚
❹ be ready to V 準備   belief 信仰
❺ potential 潛在的

1. _____

2. _____

3. _____

4. _____

5. _____

Sentence Combination 　句子合併

說明 請根據提示，將各題的兩個句子合併成一個語意通順、語法正確的英文句子。

1. as long as

We will achieve our goals.

We will never give up.

➡ _____

as long as　只要

2. with

The girl has long hair.

This girl is my sister.

➡ _____

with...　擁有

3. instead of

Bobby didn't go swimming.

Bobby stayed home watching TV.

➡ _____

instead of　而不是

4. after

Johnny finished his breakfast.

Then Johnny hurried to school.

➡ _____

5. by

Carlos won Helen's heart.

Carlos gave her a diamond ring.

➡ _____

by V-ing　藉著

Guided Translation 克漏式翻譯

說明 下面一段短文中，有數處以中文呈現，請利用上下文線索及提示（如單字、片語等）將其譯成正確、通順、達意且前後連貫的英文。

1. 本土企業，非營利基金會，還有很多其他個人捐贈了超過三億七千萬台幣 for the Cloud Gate Dance Theatre so that they could build a new rehearsal studio. The original one 2. 在 2008 年 2 月初被一把火完全摧毀。 In appreciation of the generous donations, Lin Hwai-min, founder of the Cloud Gate, 3. 承諾他們將會善用這筆捐款 because 4. 他清楚的了解到捐贈者的錢都是辛苦賺來的。 Lee Yuan-tseh, a Nobel laureate, added that although the fire destroyed most of the Cloud Gate's assets, 5. 它也帶來新的機會。

❶ local 當地的；本土的　non-profit 非營利的　foundation 基金會
❸ promised that 承諾　make the best use of/make the most of 善用
❹ be aware that 清楚了解　hard-earned 不易賺得、辛苦賺來的
❺ bring about 帶來、造成　chance/opportunity 機會、時機

1. _____

2. _____

3. _____

4. _____

5. _____

Sentence Combination 句子合併

說明 請根據提示，將各題的兩個句子合併成一個語意通順、語法正確的英文句子。

1. should

Joan had to write an English composition last Sunday.

Joan didn't do it at all.

➩ _____

_____

should have + V-en 過去該做而沒做

2. with

Alex read a Dear John letter from his girlfriend.

Tears were rolling down his face.

➩ _____

_____

with + O + OC 與…伴隨著　Dear John letter 分手信

3. what

What does Jimmy want?

Nobody knows.

➩ _____

_____

4. prefer

I like Italian food.

I don't like fast food.

➩ _____

_____

5. nor

Melky didn't concentrate in class.

Steve didn't concentrate in class, either.

➩ _____

_____

Guided Translation 克漏式翻譯

說明 下面一段短文中，有數處以中文呈現，請利用上下文線索及提示（如單字、片語等）將其譯成正確、通順、達意且前後連貫的英文。

US scientists reported that heat waves, wildfires, diseases and smog might be caused by global warming. 1. 大家都相信全球暖化是不可避免，而且人類該承擔這個責任。 2. 非常有可能全球暖化是人為的溫室氣體排放所造成的。 Experts said that extreme weather events and diseases caused by global warming can kill more people as temperatures rise. 3. 顯然地，大眾健康和氣候變遷有很大的關聯。4. 因此，全球暖化不僅威脅人類生活，而且造成一些物種絕種。 As a result, many countries worked on regulating greenhouse gas emissions. However, what is the best solution? It's quite easy for us: 5. 請節能減碳。

❶ it is believed that = S + is believed + to + V 大家都相信
　 inevitable 不可避免的　be to blame 該承擔責任
❷ it is very likely that 很有可能　be caused by 由…造成　man-made 人工的
❸ there is a strong link between A and B A 和 B 有很大的關聯
❹ not only...but also 不但…而且　extinct 絕種
❺ save/conserve 節省　carbon dioxide emissions 二氧化碳排放

1. _____

2. _____

3. _____

4. _____

5. _____

Sentence Combination 句子合併

說明 請根據提示，將各題的兩個句子合併成一個語意通順、語法正確的英文句子。

1. as soon as

I walked out of the house.

Then I witnessed a car accident.

➡ _____

witness 目擊

2. such

Miss Lin is a very famous fashion model.

Everybody knows her.

➡ _____

3. neither...nor...

Anna didn't go shopping yesterday afternoon.

Anna didn't see the movie yesterday afternoon.

➡ _____

4. for fear of

Jimmy got up at 6:00 this morning.

He was afraid that he might miss the first bus.

➡ _____

for fear of 以免

5. take

I spent three hours on the Internet.

I was searching for some information.

➡ _____

It takes sb. + 時間 + to V.... = sb. + take + 時間 + to V.... 花時間做…

Guided Translation 克漏式翻譯

說明 下面一段短文中，有數處以中文呈現，請利用上下文線索及提示（如單字、片語等）將其譯成正確、通順、達意且前後連貫的英文。

1. 由於全球經濟衰退，很多公司都在裁員。 This causes not only the unemployment rate to rise but also social problems. Some parents are out of work and 2. 他們的小孩被迫從大學休學去打工幫忙家計。 Some experts point out that this has been the greatest economic depression over the past hundred years. 3. 很多工廠倒閉，很多公司破產。 "This is sure to continue for years and 4. 這個經濟情況比我們想像的還壞三倍，" adds a joint venture CEO in Taiwan. However, 5. 我們對人生仍應抱持樂觀態度。 After all, when one door is closed, God will open another for us.

❶ due to/because of + N 由於… global 全球性的
economic recession 經濟不景氣 lay off 資遣 employee 員工
❷ drop out of school 輟學 work part-time 打工 support the family 養家
❸ close down 關閉 go bankrupt 破產
❹ three times 三次 imagine 想像
❺ hold an optimistic/pessimistic attitude toward life 對人生抱持樂觀／悲觀態度

1. _____

2. _____

3. _____

4. _____

5. _____

Sentence Combination 句子合併

說明 請根據提示，將各題的兩個句子合併成一個語意通順、語法正確的英文句子。

1. times

Macy weighs 40 kilograms.

Her father weighs 120 kilograms.

➡ _____

2. same...as

John has a new cell phone.

Mary has a new cell phone, too.

➡ _____

3. and so

Ann takes a walk in the park twice a week.

Sue takes a walk in the park twice a week, too.

➡ _____

4. The bag...

I am carrying a bag.

It is very heavy.

➡ _____

5. if

Julia is not good at math.

Julia cannot help me solve the math problem.

➡ _____

Guided Translation 克漏式翻譯

說明 下面一段短文中，有數處以中文呈現，請利用上下文線索及提示（如單字、片語等）將其譯成正確、通順、達意且前後連貫的英文。

Sometimes your friends either show their different opinions from yours or argue with you when you converse with each other. 1. 但是請保持冷靜；不要那麼容易生氣。 You should respect them. 2. 他們可能心情不好 or they just hold on to their beliefs. 3. 那並不意味著他們不喜歡你或想挑你毛病。 Since you are good friends, there must be some mutual understanding between you and your friends. 4. 試著替朋友著想，你會更好受。 As the saying goes, "A friend in need is a friend indeed." 5. 朋友不就是這樣嗎？

❶ stay/remain/keep calm 保持冷靜　get mad/angry 盛怒；抓狂
❷ be in a bad mood/be not in a good mood 心情不好
❸ not necessarily mean that 不一定意味著　pick on sb. 挑剔
❹ think for 為⋯想
❺ what are...for? ⋯代表著什麼？

1. _____

2. _____

3. _____

4. _____

5. _____

Sentence Combination 句子合併

說明 請根據提示，將各題的兩個句子合併成一個語意通順、語法正確的英文句子。

1. hear

Jenny was playing the piano in the next room.

We all heard it.

➡ _____

hear/listen to/watch/see/look at/observe ＋ O ＋ V/V-ing 感官動詞的用法

2. ...where...

Where is she going?

I have no idea.

➡ _____

3. as...as...

The black luggage weighs 40 pounds.

The red luggage weighs 40 pounds, too.

➡ _____

4. forget

I didn't wake up my brother at seven o'clock this morning.

I forgot to do it.

➡ _____

5. too...to...

David is very busy.

He can't take his children to school every day.

➡ _____

Guided Translation 克漏式翻譯

說明 下面一段短文中，有數處以中文呈現，請利用上下文線索及提示（如單字、片語等）將其譯成正確、通順、達意且前後連貫的英文。

Have you ever imagined that you win millions of dollars overnight? 1. 很多人夢想一夜致富，but only a few can make it. 2. 根據調查，那些中頭獎的人傾向什麼都要—luxury homes, expensive cars, designer clothes, etc. Eventually, they get into the habit of overspending and 3. 他們大部份人結果都一無所有。 What's worse, some even suffer from depression 4. 而且必須向專業的諮商人員求助。 So, don't envy those lottery winners. Unless they can invest their newly-acquired fortune in a better way (actually, most of them can't), 5. 他們也會在一夜之間回到從前。

❶ dream of + V-ing 夢想　get/become rich 致富　overnight 一夜之間
❷ according to/based on 根據　hit the jackpot 中頭彩　tend to 傾向；易於
❸ end up + V-ing/with + N 結果竟是
❹ turn to sb. for help 向…求助　professional counselor 專業的諮商人員
❺ used to + V 以前…

1. _____

2. _____

3. _____

4. _____

5. _____

Sentence Combination 句子合併

說明 請根據提示，將各題的兩個句子合併成一個語意通順、語法正確的英文句子。

1. V-ing

Grace did the housework all day.

It made Grace very tired.

➡

———————————————————————————

make + O + OC (Adj/V)

2. without

Johnny finished the final report by himself.

Jane did not help him.

➡

———————————————————————————

without + V-ing/N

3. in order that

A great number of high school students study very hard.

They want to enter their ideal universities.

➡

———————————————————————————

in order to V = in order that-clause 為了

4. not...until

Jenny didn't show up at the party.

Everyone was about to leave.

➡

———————————————————————————

show up 出現　be about to V 即將

5. S + V₁..., V₂ing

My father sat on the sofa.

He watched the evening news.

➡

———————————————————————————

Guided Translation 克漏式翻譯

說明 下面一段短文中，有數處以中文呈現，請利用上下文線索及提示（如單字、片語等）將其譯成正確、通順、達意且前後連貫的英文。

Some years ago, we had only three channels on TV in Taiwan. However, television technology has advanced greatly over the past twenty years. 1. 今日我們有高達一百個頻道讓我們選擇，包括有線和衛星頻道。 We used to complain that we had so few channel choices. But now there are so many channels on TV that 2. 我們一直切換頻道卻很難決定要看什麼。 People have been wondering whether TV is good or bad for us 3. 雖然電視在我們日常生活中扮演這麼重要的角色。 Positively speaking, TV offers educational and social functions. 4. 它提供重要事件的即時新聞並擴展我們的視野。 On the contrary, television can be a distraction from studying, especially for school children. What's worse, 5. 電視可能造成越來越多的犯罪和暴力 due to inappropriate content of TV programs.

❶ up to 高達　to choose from 從中選擇　satellite channels 衛星頻道
❷ keep(on) + V-ing 一直、繼續　switch the channels 切換頻道
　 have trouble/difficulty/a hard time + V-ing 不太會做⋯
❸ play an important/a vital role 扮演重要角色
❹ breaking news 即時新聞　expand/widen/broaden one's horizons 增廣視野
❺ lead to/result in/contribute to V-ing/N 導致

1. _____

2. _____

3. _____

4. _____

5. _____

Sentence Combination   句子合併

說明 請根據提示，將各題的兩個句子合併成一個語意通順、語法正確的英文句子。

1. so...that...

Wendy is very smart.

She always gets good grades in math.

➡ _____

2. as soon as

Robert got home at 5:30.

Then, he turned on the TV immediately.

➡ _____

<u>as soon as</u>/<u>the moment</u>/<u>the instant</u> $S_1 + V_1...$, $S_2 + V_2$ 一…就

3. and neither

Angelina did not keep a pet at home.

Sandra did not keep a pet at home, either.

➡ _____

neither Aux + S + V 否定倒裝

neither be + S....

4. as...as...

Marlin spends 2 hours surfing the Net every day.

Jennifer spends 2 hours surfing the Net every day, too.

➡ _____

as...as... 和…一樣　surf the Net 上網

5. V_1-ing..., S + V_2

Edward was late for school frequently.

He was often punished by his homeroom teacher.

➡ _____

homeroom teacher 導師

Guided Translation 克漏式翻譯

說明 下面一段短文中，有數處以中文呈現，請利用上下文線索及提示（如單字、片語等）將其譯成正確、通順、達意且前後連貫的英文。

Most people enjoy talking instead of listening. Yet listening is an ability that everyone should learn to possess in different degree. 1. 好的聆聽者聽的越多，他們對他們四周所發生的事情就越敏銳。 In addition, good listeners tend to tolerate others than to criticize. 2. 因此，他們比別人更少敵人，且可能變成最受喜愛的人。 However, there are exceptions to that generality. For example, 3. 雖然有些政府官員是很棒的聆聽者，但他們不受人們歡迎。 One of the most important reasons for their unpopularity is that 4. 他們只是聆聽卻沒有行動。 So, the best advice to government officials is to act now. As the proverb says: 5. 坐而言不如起而行。

❶ the more..., the more... 越…越
　 what's going on/happening/the matter 發生什麼事
❷ fewer + 複數 N　較少
❸ official 官員　be popular with 受歡迎
❹ without 沒有…　merely/only/simply 只是

1. _____

2. _____

3. _____

4. _____

5. _____

Sentence Combination 句子合併

說明 請根據提示，將各題的兩個句子合併成一個語意通順、語法正確的英文句子。

1. such...that...

Daniel is very energetic.

He can play sports all day without taking a break.

➡ _____

take a break 休息

2. with

The little boy is looking at the chocolate.

His mouth is watering.

➡ _____

with + O + OC (V-ing/V-en)

3. there

There are 20 students at the bus stop.

They are waiting for the bus.

➡ _____

4. would rather...than...

I like staying home on Sundays.

I don't like going out shopping on Sundays.

➡ _____

5. V-ing

David felt tired this morning.

He fell asleep in class this morning.

➡ _____

V_1-ing..., S + V_2.... （分詞構句） fall asleep 睡著

Guided Translation 克漏式翻譯

說明 下面一段短文中，有數處以中文呈現，請利用上下文線索及提示（如單字、片語等）將其譯成正確、通順、達意且前後連貫的英文。

The "30-Hour Famine," sponsored by World Vision, 1. 是個國際性對抗飢餓活動。 It aims to make participants starve themselves for 30 hours 2. 以便清楚瞭解飢餓是怎麼一回事。 During the 30 hours, they do fund-raising and different activities. 3. 這使人們能對抗世界饑餓和貧窮 while saving lives and providing hope. When a friend asked me if I wanted to take part in the program by making myself hungry for 30 hours, 4. 我在想他到底在談什麼， so I didn't take it seriously. After finishing the program, 5. 我了解如果我們現在採取行動，我們就能阻止世界饑餓 because a little bit of money can make a big difference.

❶ an international...program 國際性…活動　hunger-fighting 對抗飢餓
❷ ...so that... 以便於　a clear understanding of... 清楚瞭解…
❸ enable...to V 使…能　to fight against 對抗　poverty 貧窮
❹ what on earth/in the world 究竟是怎麼
❺ realize that 了解到…　take action 採取行動

1. _____

2. _____

3. _____

4. _____

5. _____

Sentence Combination 句子合併

說明 請根據提示，將各題的兩個句子合併成一個語意通順、語法正確的英文句子。

1. with

An old man sat on the bench in the park.

He closed his eyes.

 _____

2. lest

Jane got up early in the morning.

She did that in order not to be late for school.

➟ _____

...lest + S + should V 以免

3. whose

Brad married a 25-year-old beautiful girl.

Her father is a history professor at Harvard University.

➟ _____

4. so

My father has seen *Cape No.7* four times.

Tom's father has seen *Cape No.7* four times, too.

➟ _____

so + be/Aux + S 肯定倒裝

5. upon

Allen heard a funny joke.

He burst into laughter right away.

➟ _____

upon/on + V-ing 一…就　burst into laughter 大笑

Guided Translation 克漏式翻譯

說明 下面一段短文中，有數處以中文呈現，請利用上下文線索及提示（如單字、片語等）將其譯成正確、通順、達意且前後連貫的英文。

Big cities are crowded and filled with noises and pollution. 1. 大都市忙碌的生活型態正損害著人們的心靈。 People in big cities seldom notice or interact with their fellow citizens. 2. 即使他們每天被上百人包圍，仍覺得孤單。 As a result, many city people dream of simpler and more relaxing lives in the country. 3. 不過，那些搬到鄉下的人需要調整生活方式及心態。 In the countryside, 4. 他們覺得很難擁有在大都市被視為是理所當然的便利。 Even driving to a convenience store can take them 40 minutes. 5. 很不幸地，有些人無法忍受這樣的鄉下生活而決定再次搬回大都市。

❶ busy lifestyle 忙碌的生活型態　 damage 損害
❷ even though 即使　 be surrounded by 圍繞著、包圍著
❸ make an adjustment to 調整…　 attitude 態度
❹ find it hard to V 覺得…很難　 choices 選擇　 convenience 便利
　 take... for granted 視…為理所當然
❺ can't stand + V-ing 無法忍受…　 lead a life 過生活　 move back to 搬回

1. _____

2. _____

3. _____

4. _____

5. _____

Sentence Combination 　句子合併

說明 請根據提示，將各題的兩個句子合併成一個語意通順、語法正確的英文句子。

1. neither...nor...

Andy did not concentrate in class.

He did not do well in extracurricular activities, either.

➩ _____

do well in 在…表現好　extracurricular activities 課外活動

2. despite

Fred's doctor warned him.

Fred still did not quit smoking.

➩ _____

despite V-ing/N 雖然　quit + V-ing 戒除…

3. lead to

It snowed heavily last night.

The power failure happened last night.

➩ _____

lead to/result in/contribute to 導致　power failure 停電

4. after

Gina ate her breakfast at 6:00.

Then she went to school by bike.

➩ _____

5. Only when

People do not realize the importance of health.

They do only when they lose it.

➩ _____

only when... Aux + S + V （only 在句首時，句子需要倒裝。）

only when... be + S....

Guided Translation 克漏式翻譯

說明 下面一段短文中，有數處以中文呈現，請利用上下文線索及提示（如單字、片語等）將其譯成正確、通順、達意且前後連貫的英文。

Many people reach out for the newspaper every morning seemingly to find out the latest news in the world. 1. 事實上有些人只是對名人，像是歌手、電影明星或政治人物的八卦有興趣。 A great part of what they know depends on reporters' stories. However, 2. 記者能被信任到何種程度？ Sometimes facts are easy to clarify, but at other times, reporters also have to count on their judgment. 3. 為了滿足讀者，記者報導一些像是名人誹聞、性醜聞之類的令人難堪的事件， which usually have nothing to do with public interest. Some reporters invade people's privacy just to get another sensational story. 4. 誰知道新聞倫理與言論自由的界線在哪裡？ If reporters keep hunting for gossips, 5. 他們最後會落的一無所有，且沒人會再相信他們。

❶ take interest in/be interested in 對…感興趣　such as 像是…之類
　gossip 八卦　celebrity 名人　politician 政治人物
❷ to what extent 到某種程度　reporter/journalist 記者
❸ cover/report/write （新聞）報導　love affair 誹聞　sex scandal 性醜聞
❹ boundary 界線　journalism ethics 新聞倫理　freedom of speech 言論自由
❺ end up with + N/V-ing 結果、後來…

1. _____

2. _____

3. _____

4. _____

5. _____

Sentence Combination 句子合併

說明 請根據提示，將各題的兩個句子合併成一個語意通順、語法正確的英文句子。

1. in which

The book was about gardening.

I took great interest in the book.

▷ _____

2. with + O + OC

Brian was sitting on the sofa.

His eyes were wide open.

▷ _____

3. While...,

John is mopping the floor.

John's wife is busy cooking in the kitchen.

▷ _____

4. one of...

I have many good friends.

Allen is my good friend.

▷ _____

5. too...to...

My grandpa is very old.

My grandpa cannot walk fast.

▷ _____

Guided Translation 克漏式翻譯

說明 下面一段短文中，有數處以中文呈現，請利用上下文線索及提示（如單字、片語等）將其譯成正確、通順、達意且前後連貫的英文。

When you were young, your parents and teachers taught you how to act properly. They demonstrated good manners 1. 且解釋哪些行為無法被接受。 However, those behaviors are not all universal. 2. 每個文化有它自己的禁忌習俗及規範 about what is right and what is wrong. The most important is to 3. 尊重每個文化且公平地對待它。 For example, in some cultures, it is very bad manners to ask an adult how old he/she is. 4. 在其他文化裡，政治、宗教和性也可能是禁忌的話題。 Besides, long pauses are considered uncomfortable and should be avoided. People would think that 5. 你不想跟他們講話，如果你沉默太久的話。 In a word, learn as many cultural practices as you can so that you won't offend your friends.

❶ acceptable 可接受的
❷ taboo 禁忌　custom 習俗　rule 規定、規則、規範
❸ treat 對待　fairly 公平地
❹ politics 政治　religion 宗教　topic/subject 話題、題材
❺ feel like V-ing/would like to V （不）想要

1. _____

2. _____

3. _____

4. _____

5. _____

Sentence Combination 句子合併

說明 請根據提示，將各題的兩個句子合併成一個語意通順、語法正確的英文句子。

1. if

Will Steve arrive on time?

I wonder that.

➡ _____

on time 準時

2. make

George washes dishes for his mother.

George's mother always makes him do it.

➡ _____

make + O + V/Adj 使役動詞用法

3. when

Fred got promoted in June.

His wife was laid off in June.

➡ _____

get promoted 晉升　lay off 資遣

4. see

I saw Grace in the next room.

Grace was watching TV in the next room.

➡ _____

hear/listen to/watch/see/look at/observe + O + V/V-ing

5. be used to

I eat night snacks before going to bed.

I have been used to it.

➡ _____

be used to N/V-ing 習慣；適應

Guided Translation 克漏式翻譯

說明 下面一段短文中，有數處以中文呈現，請利用上下文線索及提示（如單字、片語等）將其譯成正確、通順、達意且前後連貫的英文。

Obesity is one of the fastest growing health problems in the world. According to the World Health Organization, 1. 世上每四個人中就有一個過胖。 Being overweight gets the better chance of developing diabetes, heart disease, and certain cancers, etc. 2. 越來越多人每天離家長時間工作。 We take a car, bus, or train to work instead of walking or biking. 3. 所以由於缺乏運動我們很容易變胖。 In addition, we return home from work after a tiring day and 4. 我們太忙而無法好好準備健康的一餐，以至於趕忙吃速食就當晚餐。 Day after day, we get too much fat and become obese. But what is the best solution? Experts suggest that 5. 我們儘可能多吃蔬菜、水果，且有足夠的休息和運動。 Do you want to lose weight? Please do as the experts say.

---

❶ one out of every... 每…個…中有一個　overweight 過胖
❷ far from 遠離
❸ due to/owing to/because of/as a result of 由於；因為　lack of 缺乏
❹ too busy to V 太忙而無法　grab 趕緊（吃）
❺ as (many/much)...as possible 儘可能…

---

1. _____

2. _____

3. _____

4. _____

5. _____

Sentence Combination 句子合併

說明 請根據提示，將各題的兩個句子合併成一個語意通順、語法正確的英文句子。

1. by

David's father sells fruit at the roadside.

He makes a lot of money.

➡ _____

2. without

Peter didn't say a word.

Peter left the room.

➡ _____

without V-ing/N

3. since

Liz started living in the Uuited States three years ago.

She is still living in the Uuited States now.

➡ _____

4. while

Cindy fell asleep in the study.

Jenny was doing her homework then.

➡ _____

5. It is

Andy tries to find a job.

Finding a job is difficult.

➡ _____

It is + Adj + for + sb. + to V

Guided Translation 克漏式翻譯

說明 下面一段短文中，有數處以中文呈現，請利用上下文線索及提示（如單字、片語等）將其譯成正確、通順、達意且前後連貫的英文。

When we have a fever, we usually panic. However, 1. 我們應學會與發燒相處，雖然它使我們不舒服。 Our body temperature varies from one moment to the next throughout the day, and 2. 我們的正常體溫應在 37°C 左右。 If our body temperature passes the 37.5°C mark, it means we have a fever. 3. 簡單說，我們把發燒當疾病。 But actually, it isn't. 4. 發燒通常是某種疾病的警訊。 Any sickness can cause our body temperature to rise. When fever strikes, 5. 先洗個溫水澡和喝足夠的水。 If it still doesn't work, going to the doctor at once is the best solution.

❶ get along with 相處
❷ body temperature 體溫　degrees Celsius 攝氏
❸ in short/in a word/to sum up 簡而言之
　 think of/view/see/regard...as 視…為　illness/infection/sickness 疾病
❹ signal/warning 警訊
❺ take a bath 洗澡

1. _____

2. _____

3. _____

4. _____

5. _____

Sentence Combination 句子合併

說明 請根據提示，將各題的兩個句子合併成一個語意通順、語法正確的英文句子。

1. and

The firefighters arrived.

They put out the fire.

➡ _____

put out/extinguish 撲滅

2. where

We stayed at a hotel last night.

The hotel was near the MRT station.

➡ _____

3. or

Get up early.

You will be late for school.

➡ _____

4. before

You cross the road.

You always have to look both ways.

➡ _____

look both ways 看兩邊

5. but

Linda is hungry.

Linda does not have anything to eat.

➡ _____

Guided Translation 克漏式翻譯

說明 下面一段短文中，有數處以中文呈現，請利用上下文線索及提示（如單字、片語等）將其譯成正確、通順、達意且前後連貫的英文。

A growing number of children play computer games in their free time. However, 1. 父母和老師擔心打電動對他們有害。 Adults, especially teachers, believe that students' violent behavior is closely related to playing computer games. But according to research, 2. 打電動只是浪費時間，且與壞行為毫無關係。 Parents could feel relieved and don't need to worry too much. 3. 只要父母能限制小孩打電動的時間， moderate use of video games can also be positive. What's more, 4. 有些專家指出打電動可能跟運動一樣有益。 That is, playing computer games can help let out extra energy and relieve pressure. 5. 最重要的是適量。 That's what parents and teachers should be concerned about.

❶ be concerned about + N/ that-clause 關心、擔心顧慮
　 do harm to...= do...harm 對⋯造成傷害
❷ a waste of time 浪費時間　 have nothing to do with 與⋯無關
❸ as long as 只要　 amount of time 時間
❹ indicate 指出　 as...as 和⋯一樣
❺ the most important of all 最重要的是⋯

1. _____

2. _____

3. _____

4. _____

5. _____

Sentence Combination 句子合併

說明 請根據提示，將各題的兩個句子合併成一個語意通順、語法正確的英文句子。

1. without

My mom went out yesterday morning.

She didn't lock the door.

➡ _____

without V-ing/N

2. be good at

My brother always tells ghost stories.

He is good at it.

➡ _____

be good/skillful at V-ing 擅長

3. by

John went to the supermarket.

He rode a bicycle there.

➡ _____

by + 交通工具 (bicycle/car/bus/plane/train) 搭乘…

4. behind

Colin is standing behind Lucy.

He is making faces at Lucy.

➡ _____

make faces at 做鬼臉

5. what

I have no idea of it.

What is his real name?

➡ _____

have no idea = not know at all 不知道

Guided Translation 克漏式翻譯

說明 下面一段短文中，有數處以中文呈現，請利用上下文線索及提示（如單字、片語等）將其譯成正確、通順、達意且前後連貫的英文。

Every year in Taiwan, traffic accidents cause tremendous deaths. 1. 以下是造成車禍的原因。 First, drivers do not concentrate while driving. 2. 他們心不在焉且闖紅燈。 They hit the pedestrians, bike or motorbike riders just because of their inattention. Second, 3. 用路者沒有注意號誌或遵守交通規則。 They sometimes crash into each other and some of them get killed or injured. Third, 4. 某些車禍的造成是因為酒醉駕駛。 Some drivers drive home after drinking a lot of alcohol. They are unconscious while driving. After they come to themselves, tragedies have happened. Therefore, to ensure road safety, 5. 我們相信交通安全人人有責。

---

❶ the following is/are 以下是⋯
❷ absent-minded 心不在焉　run a/the red light 闖紅燈
❸ pay attention to 注意　road signs 路標　obey/follow/abide by 遵守
❹ happen/occur 造成、發生　drunk driving 酒駕
❺ be everybody's business 每個人的責任

---

1. _____

2. _____

3. _____

4. _____

5. _____

Sentence Combination 句子合併

說明 請根據提示，將各題的兩個句子合併成一個語意通順、語法正確的英文句子。

1. for

He began working on the computer four hours ago.

He is still working on it now.

➜ _____

2. ...because...

My wife and I didn't go to the party.

Sally didn't invite us.

➜ _____

3. so

Mark didn't study hard for the entrance exam.

He didn't pass the entrance exam.

➜ _____

4. nor

Wilson never hit the jackpot.

I never hit the jackpot, either.

➜ _____

5. if

My sister wants to go to the cinema tonight.

I am wondering it.

➜ _____

Guided Translation 克漏式翻譯

說明 下面一段短文中，有數處以中文呈現，請利用上下文線索及提示（如單字、片語等）將其譯成正確、通順、達意且前後連貫的英文。

The standard of living varies from one country to another. Unfortunately, 1. 即使在富有的國家，仍然有很多流浪漢。 Without a doubt, economic recession is one of the main causes which make so many people homeless. An increasing number of people 2. 失業且付不起房租。 Day after day, they wander and live on the streets. 3. 有些流浪漢有精神疾病且沒有人可以照顧他們。 They are the worst ones and may cause serious social problems. Other homeless people 4. 可能只是跟父母意見不合後就離家。 They are so young that they have to be paid most attention to. Although 5. 慈善團體和教會提供臨時庇護所和食物給這些流浪漢， yet the government authorities should take action to help them go back to their normal life.

❶ even 即使　homeless 無家可歸的
❷ be out of job/become jobless 失業　afford to V/N 負擔
❸ mentally ill 精神疾病　take care of/look after 照顧
❹ have a disagreement with 與…意見不合
❺ charities 慈善團體　makeshift/temporary 暫時的

1. _____

2. _____

3. _____

4. _____

5. _____

Sentence Combination 句子合併

說明 請根據提示，將各題的兩個句子合併成一個語意通順、語法正確的英文句子。

1. since

Barbara felt sick yesterday morning.

She is still sick now.

➡ _____

2. neither...nor...

Roger didn't steal his Dad's money.

Roger didn't break into his neighbor's house.

➡ _____

3. ...who

Who lives in the next house?

I don't know about that.

➡ _____

4. take

I walked to the main station.

I spent one hour on it.

➡ _____

It takes sb. + 時間 + to V = sb. + takes + 時間 + to V　花時間做…

5. ...although...

A severe typhoon came.

The authorities didn't close the bridge.

➡ _____

Guided Translation 克漏式翻譯

說明 下面一段短文中，有數處以中文呈現，請利用上下文線索及提示（如單字、片語等）將其譯成正確、通順、達意且前後連貫的英文。

How people face trouble or difficulties differs a lot. 1. 有些人有麻煩時看起來很鬱悶。 We can easily notice those people at first sight. 2. 也有人看起來仍很快樂且抱持樂觀態度 when they are in the low point of their life. This kind of people are popular with their friends 3. 因為他們總是帶給別人快樂。 Still others show no sign of any emotional changes in their faces. 4. 我們很難從他們的臉上表情觀察出任何異樣。 In a word, there are ups and downs in life and 5. 人們偶而會經歷困境。 No matter how you feel, time still flies and days go by. Why not make yourself happy and make others happy as well?

❶ look down 看起來鬱悶　be in trouble 有麻煩
❷ hold an optimistic attitude 抱持樂觀態度
❹ facial expressions 臉部表情
❺ hard times 困苦　one time or another/once in a while 偶而

1. _____

2. _____

3. _____

4. _____

5. _____

Sentence Combination 句子合併

說明 請根據提示，將各題的兩個句子合併成一個語意通順、語法正確的英文句子。

1. instead of

Paul likes to read at home.

Paul doesn't like to go to the movies.

➡ _____

2. ..., one of...

Powell has seven digital cameras.

One of the digital cameras is made in Germany.

➡ _____

3. lest

Donna studies hard day and night.

She doesn't want to fail the exam.

➡ _____

4. ...such...that...

Miss Lin is very beautiful.

A lot of handsome young men want to be her boyfriends.

➡ _____

5. if

Diana is not John.

She cannot imagine how miserable John's life is.

➡ _____

Guided Translation 克漏式翻譯

說明 下面一段短文中，有數處以中文呈現，請利用上下文線索及提示（如單字、片語等）將其譯成正確、通順、達意且前後連貫的英文。

Every year, Lunar New Year comes in late January or early February. 1. *每年的這個時候，傳統市場擠滿了人。* People return to their hometowns to have family reunions. Especially 2. *他們會在除夕時吃一頓團圓大餐。* After the feast, parents usually give red envelopes to their family members, 3. *希望來年給他們帶來好運。* On New Year's Day, particularly in the countryside, 4. *大人通常去拜訪親戚朋友而小孩喜歡放鞭炮，* which according to the old tradition, means scaring evil ghosts away. Most important of all, 5. *每人至少有七天的假期，* in which they can relax and have fun.

---

❶ at the time of... 在⋯的時候
 be full of/be filled with/be crowded with 擠滿
❷ Lunar New Year's Eve 除夕　 feast 大餐　 reunion 團聚
❸ bring good luck to 帶來好運
❹ set off/let off 燃放

---

1. _____

2. _____

3. _____

4. _____

5. _____

Sentence Combination 句子合併

說明 請根據提示，將各題的兩個句子合併成一個語意通順、語法正確的英文句子。

1. not only...but also...

Angelina is beautiful.

Angelina is attractive.

↪ _____

2. whose

Harry always listens carefully in class.

Harry's attention is never distracted.

↪ _____

3. ...when

People make resolutions on January 1st on the lunar calendar.

The Chinese New Year begins on January 1st on the lunar calendar.

↪ _____

4. if

You study harder.

You can do better in the entrance exam.

↪ _____

5. if

Morris was not innocent.

Morris was put in prison for 3 years.

↪ _____

Guided Translation 克漏式翻譯

說明 下面一段短文中，有數處以中文呈現，請利用上下文線索及提示（如單字、片語等）將其譯成正確、通順、達意且前後連貫的英文。

Over the past few years, the global climate has changed a lot. 1. 某些從不下雪的地方突然下大雪。 Heavy rain floods areas where it used to rain once in a while. 2. 雖然全世界的領袖定期碰面來討論此一嚴重議題， yet no consensus has been reached so far. Experts point out that 3. 解決方法之一就是減少溫室氣體的排放。 However, the problem is that some leading countries refuse to sign the agreement to cut carbon dioxide emissions. 4. 這個環保政策一定會造成工業工廠的利潤損失， especially in the US. Thus, those regular meetings of world leaders 5. 結果只是漫無目的的演講和辯論而已。

---

❷ all around the world 全球的、全世界的　issue 議題
❸ cut down/reduce/decrease 減少　greenhouse gas 溫室氣體
　emissions 排放
❹ environmental protection 環保　policy 政策　profit 利潤
❺ turn out to be 結果是　aimless 漫無目的的

---

1. _____

2. _____

3. _____

4. _____

5. _____

Sentence Combination 句子合併

說明 請根據提示，將各題的兩個句子合併成一個語意通順、語法正確的英文句子。

1. unless

You don't get up early.

You can't catch the first bus.

 _____

2. as a result of

It snowed heavily.

The soccer game was postponed.

_____

3. so

Amanda is tall and charming.

Sandy is tall and charming, too.

_____

4. as...as...

I saw three movies last month.

Stanley saw three movies last month, too.

_____

5. which

I borrowed four books from the library.

I was interested in the four books.

_____

Guided Translation 克漏式翻譯

說明 下面一段短文中，有數處以中文呈現，請利用上下文線索及提示（如單字、片語等）將其譯成正確、通順、達意且前後連貫的英文。

Every year in Taiwan, as temperatures get higher in summer, 1. 全島常有溺水的報導。 Sadly enough, no one really pays attention to the dangers they will face when going swimming. Those drowning cases seldom happened in swimming pools, 2. 而是在人們根本不應該去游泳的河流。 They ignore the warning signs and directly jump into the river, 3. 結果頭撞到水底下的岩石而失去生命。 Owing to the numerous tragedies every year, 4. 有人建議警方應加強巡邏並設立更多的警告牌。 However, it doesn't seem to be a good way to prevent people from getting drowned. 5. 有效的方法之一就是政府應蓋更多的游泳池 and ban people from swimming in the rivers.

---

❶ get drowned 溺水　around the island 全島
❷ be not supposed to V （不）應該
❸ end up + V-ing/with + N 結果　crash 碰撞
❹ reinforce 強化　patrol 巡邏　put up 豎立　warning sign 警告標示
❺ effective 有效的

---

1. _____

2. _____

3. _____

4. _____

5. _____

Sentence Combination 句子合併

說明 請根據提示，將各題的兩個句子合併成一個語意通順、語法正確的英文句子。

1. in order to

My father gets up early in the morning.

He has to take me to school.

➡ _____

2. too...to...

Nick walked very slowly.

Nick didn't catch up with us.

➡ _____

3. upon

Justin got home in the evening.

Justin turned on the TV right away.

➡ _____

4. senior to...

Wilson is 54 years old.

Megan is 63 years old.

➡ _____

5. cost

I spent NT$200.

I bought the book.

➡ _____

Guided Translation 克漏式翻譯

說明 下面一段短文中，有數處以中文呈現，請利用上下文線索及提示（如單字、片語等）將其譯成正確、通順、達意且前後連貫的英文。

Taiwan used to be one of four "Asian tigers." 1. 它的經濟情況曾經是台灣人的驕傲 and envy of the rest of the world. Nevertheless, things have changed. According to various studies and surveys, 2. 台灣正逐漸變成所謂的 M 型社會 and it continues to move in this direction. 3. 也就是說，富者愈富，貧者愈貧。 More importantly, Taiwan's middle class is shrinking. 4. 更糟的是，失業率一直攀升 and more and more people are working longer hours for less money. 5. 這真的是我們政府應正視的問題。

❶ economical condition 經濟情況
❷ so-called 所謂的　M-shaped society M 型社會
❸ that is 也就是說
❹ what's worse 更糟的是　unemployment rate 失業率
❺ take (sth.) seriously 正視

1. _____

2. _____

3. _____

4. _____

5. _____

Sentence Combination 句子合併

說明 請根據提示，將各題的兩個句子合併成一個語意通順、語法正確的英文句子。

1. where

My mom went to the supermarket.

My mom did the shopping there.

➡ _____

2. before

I say good night to my parents.

Then, I go to bed.

➡ _____

3. make

Raymond washes his father's car twice a week.

Raymond's father makes him do it.

➡ _____

4. in spite of

The government is still planning to build another nuclear plant.

There is much opposition.

➡ _____

5. to one's surprise

I was surprised at the news.

Jenny got first place in the English speech contest.

➡ _____

Guided Translation 克漏式翻譯

說明 下面一段短文中，有數處以中文呈現，請利用上下文線索及提示（如單字、片語等）將其譯成正確、通順、達意且前後連貫的英文。

Obesity is one of the problems that school children are facing nowadays. 1. 越來越多的學童過胖 and it has become a major health issue in Taiwan. Parents, teachers, and government authorities are all concerned about this growing problem 2. 因為肥胖可能導致未來一些疾病，such as heart disease or diabetes. One of the reasons why schoolchildren get too fat is that they lack exercise. 3. 由於太多功課和太常考試，他們幾乎沒有時間運動。 Another cause is that they grab too much fast food, 4. 包括含大量卡路里的薯條、汽水和漢堡。 However, it is not school children that are to blame. One best way to help students lose weight is that 5. 父母每一餐都準備健康的食物給他們的小孩吃。

❶ overweight 過胖
❷ obesity 肥胖　result in/lead to 導致
❸ owing to/due to/because of 由於，因為　hardly 幾乎很少
❹ calories 卡路里
❺ each and every 每一個（強調用法）

1. _____

2. _____

3. _____

4. _____

5. _____

Sentence Combination 句子合併

說明 請根據提示，將各題的兩個句子合併成一個語意通順、語法正確的英文句子。

1. as soon as

Joseph heard the news of his father's death.

Joseph burst into tears.

 _____

2. nevertheless

It snowed heavily outside.

Peter went camping as usual.

 _____

3. so

Jack played golf last weekend.

Scott played golf last weekend, too.

 _____

4. prefer...to...

Roger enjoys surfing the Net.

Roger enjoys reading novels more.

 _____

5. if

The weather will be fine tomorrow.

We will go picnicking tomorrow.

_____

Guided Translation 克漏式翻譯

說明 下面一段短文中，有數處以中文呈現，請利用上下文線索及提示（如單字、片語等）將其譯成正確、通順、達意且前後連貫的英文。

It is commonly seen that 1. 青少年在散步、搭捷運或準備考試時戴上他們的 MP3 隨身聽。 Undoubtedly, MP3 players are popular; however, 2. 用 MP3 隨身聽聽太久音樂可能對聽力造成很大的傷害。 That's because in order to enjoy the stereo sound effect, listeners usually turn the volume up as loud as it goes. 3. 漸漸地他們習慣這種噪音， and according to research, they usually do not notice it. 4. 因此，下次聽 MP3 隨身聽時轉小聲。 To sum up, if you want to enjoy listening to your favorite songs in the future, 5. 現在就要好好照顧你的耳朵。

> ❷ cause damage to 對…造成傷害
> ❹ turn down/up 轉小/大聲
> ❺ take good care of 好好照顧…

1. _____

2. _____

3. _____

4. _____

5. _____

Sentence Combination 　句子合併

說明 請根據提示，將各題的兩個句子合併成一個語意通順、語法正確的英文句子。

1. would rather...than...

Mandy likes going to the library.

Mandy likes watching TV at home better.

➡ _____

2. by

He went to Tainan yesterday.

He took a bus there.

➡ _____

3. which

I got a letter.

It was written in English.

➡ _____

4. both

Cathy is charming.

Cathy is beautiful, too.

➡ _____

5. not only...but also...

Craig cooked dinner yesterday evening.

Craig washed clothes yesterday evening.

➡ _____

Guided Translation 克漏式翻譯

說明　下面一段短文中，有數處以中文呈現，請利用上下文線索及提示（如單字、片語等）將其譯成正確、通順、達意且前後連貫的英文。

Many people skip breakfast just because 1. 他們要不是沒時間吃或者是沒養成吃早餐的習慣。　Even though most people understand that breakfast is the most important meal of the day, 2. 幾乎百分之四十的人沒吃早餐就去上班或上學。Recent studies show that those who usually eat breakfast tend to keep healthy and stay fit. 3. 相反的，通常沒吃早餐的人容易變胖。Surprisingly enough, studies also reveal that 4. 有吃早餐的人比那些沒吃早餐的人課業表現較好。　In addition, 5. 早餐吃得飽使人思考更有邏輯且記憶力更好。　People actually benefit a lot from eating breakfast. Let's eat breakfast every day.

> ❶ get into the habit of　養成…的習慣
> ❸ on the contrary　相反地　　gain weight　變胖、重
> ❹ have better academic performance　有較好的課業表現
> ❺ enable...to + V　使…能夠　　think more logically　更有邏輯思考

1. _____

2. _____

3. _____

4. _____

5. _____

 Sentence Combination 句子合併

說明 請根據提示，將各題的兩個句子合併成一個語意通順、語法正確的英文句子。

1. where

Would you please tell me about that?

Where is the bus station?

➡ _____

2. ...in order to...

Wendy goes jogging every morning.

She wants to lose weight.

➡ _____

3. despite

Wilson worked very hard.

He failed the exam.

➡ _____

4. otherwise

You had better work on your report soon.

You will not meet the deadline.

➡ _____

5. not...until...

Roger didn't realize the importance of health.

Roger had a heart attack.

➡ _____

Guided Translation 克漏式翻譯

說明 下面一段短文中，有數處以中文呈現，請利用上下文線索及提示（如單字、片語等）將其譯成正確、通順、達意且前後連貫的英文。

In Taiwan, 1. <u>放天燈不僅是個受歡迎的民俗活動</u> but also considered a custom at Lantern Festival. 2. <u>傳說在過去，盜匪時常入侵村莊，</u> so villagers ran hiding in high mountains. 3. <u>他們會搶奪村民的財產，留下空盪盪的村莊。</u> After the robbers were gone, 4. <u>村長們會施放天燈來告訴村民</u> that it was safe and they could come back home. Year after year, launching sky lanterns became a custom, 5. <u>這意味著傳達願望給眾神以及表現和平。</u>

---

❶ sky lantern 天燈　folklore activity 民俗活動
❷ Legend has it that 根據傳說　robber 盜匪　invade 入侵
❸ rob + sb. + of + sth. 搶奪　belongings/properties/possession 財產
　 leave + sth. + Adj 留下⋯
❹ village head 村長　launch 施放
❺ convey...to 傳達，傳遞

---

1. _____

2. _____

3. _____

4. _____

5. _____

Sentence Combination 句子合併

說明 請根據提示，將各題的兩個句子合併成一個語意通順、語法正確的英文句子。

1. named

A mountaineer got lost in the mountains last week.

His name is Fred Johnson.

 _____

2. or

You don't follow the doctor's advice.

You won't get healthy.

➡ _____

3. ...more/Adj-er...more/Adj-er...

You study hard.

You may get good grades.

➡ _____

4. there

There are 20 students at the bus stop.

They are waiting for the bus.

➡ _____

5. so that

Andy studies Russian four hours a day.

Andy wants to study in Russia some day.

➡ _____

Guided Translation 克漏式翻譯

說明 下面一段短文中，有數處以中文呈現，請利用上下文線索及提示（如單字、片語等）將其譯成正確、通順、達意且前後連貫的英文。

A pair of giant pandas from China settled into their new home at Taipei Zoo. 1. 他們似乎情況很好 and are used to the weather here in Taipei. During Lunar New Year, both the pandas made their debut, and 2. 好幾萬人排隊就為了看這兩隻可愛的動物。 As Taipei's new celebrities, 3. 他們在終年有空調的環境裡享用竹子大餐。 They really make themselves at home and also 4. 讓動物園其他動物很羨慕。 The pandas brought Taipei City to life on Lunar New Year holidays, 5. 因為我們已經很久沒在這時候看到動物園有這麼多人。

❶ in good condition 狀況良好

❷ stand/wait in line 排隊

❸ bamboo 竹子　year-round 終年的　air-conditioned 安裝空調的

❹ jealous 忌妒、羨慕

1. _____

2. _____

3. _____

4. _____

5. _____

Sentence Combination 句子合併

說明 請根據提示，將各題的兩個句子合併成一個語意通順、語法正確的英文句子。

1. such...that

Chien-ming Wang is a wonderful pitcher.

He has a lot of fans in Taiwan.

➡ _____

2. what

I don't have any idea of it at all.

What is Lucy's address?

➡ _____

3. V-ing...,

Bob succeeded in the college entrance exam.

Bob decided to have a study tour in the US.

➡ _____

4. neither...nor

Alice didn't watch the soap opera last night.

Nick didn't watch the soap opera last night.

➡ _____

5. otherwise

You don't apologize to David.

You will be punished by your homeroom teacher.

➡ _____

Guided Translation 克漏式翻譯

說明 下面一段短文中，有數處以中文呈現，請利用上下文線索及提示（如單字、片語等）將其譯成正確、通順、達意且前後連貫的英文。

E-mail is a convenient invention which many people use every day to communicate with their friends or colleagues. I am no exception. 1. 我放學回家後，家裡一個人也沒有。 I use e-mail to contact my parents in their offices. 2. 看他們的 e-mail 比接到他們的電話還有趣。 By writing e-mail, I no longer feel bored when I am home alone. Besides, 3. 透過電子郵件我能夠跟住在遠方的朋友聯絡。 I neither spend a lot of money on long-distance calls 4. 也不用等朋友好幾天才能回信給我。 E-mail is really helpful and has many benefits. 5. 它既省時又省錢。

❷ read/check email 查看電子郵件
❸ keep/stay in touch with 與…保持聯絡　far away/in the distance 遠方
❹ write back 回信
❺ both...and... 既…又…

1. _____

2. _____

3. _____

4. _____

5. _____

Sentence Combination 句子合併

説明 請根據提示，將各題的兩個句子合併成一個語意通順、語法正確的英文句子。

1. while

It started to rain.

We were playing basketball.

2. so that

My brother works hard.

He wants to make more money.

3. those who

Those people are healthy.

They often exercise regularly.

4. which

The National Palace Museum attracts a lot of foreign tourists.

It is one of the must-go spots in Taipei.

5. besides

Nancy enjoys writing stories.

Nancy enjoys making movies.

Guided Translation 克漏式翻譯

說明 下面一段短文中，有數處以中文呈現，請利用上下文線索及提示（如單字、片語等）將其譯成正確、通順、達意且前後連貫的英文。

According to research, school children in Taiwan watch TV at least two hours every day. 1. 體重過重的孩童現在是越來越多了。 But what's the relation between watching TV and getting overweight? Experts point out that 2. 看電視時不吃零食的小孩微乎其微。 That is, most children watch TV and eat snacks unconsciously at the same time. 3. 更糟的是，這些垃圾食物含有大量的脂肪、糖及鹽分， which always make people overweight. 4. 孩子電視看得越多，他們就變得越胖。 So, one of the best ways to stop children from getting overweight is to 5. 減少他們看電視的時間以少吃零食。

❶ more and more 越來越多的　overweight 過胖的
❷ few 微乎其微的
❸ what's worse 更糟的是　fat 脂肪　salt 鹽、鹽分
❹ junk food 垃圾食物　be rich in 富含/具有大量的
❺ cut down on/reduce 減少…的量

1. _____

2. _____

3. _____

4. _____

5. _____

Sentence Combination 句子合併

說明 請根據提示，將各題的兩個句子合併成一個語意通順、語法正確的英文句子。

1. who

I love to talk to Dr. Lin.

He is very kind and knowledgeable.

 _____

2. so...that

Morris is very lucky.

Morris has hit the jackpot two times.

 _____

3. Not only...but also

Local people enjoy sending sky lanterns into the sky.

Visitors admire the wonderful celebration.

 _____

4. V-ing...,

Angela saw her parents at the airport.

Angela cried and ran to her parents.

 _____

5. inferior

The black backpack is of good quality.

The green backpack is of bad quality.

 _____

Guided Translation 克漏式翻譯

說明 下面一段短文中，有數處以中文呈現，請利用上下文線索及提示（如單字、片語等）將其譯成正確、通順、達意且前後連貫的英文。

Pets are believed to be humans' best friends. However, 1. 人類真的是寵物的好朋友嗎？ Sometimes the answer is "No." According to a study in the United States, 2. 當人類面臨財務問題時，易於拋棄他們的寵物。 But pets are always faithful to their owners all their lifetime. 3. 寵物與主人分享快樂悲傷， but pet owners abandon their pets if necessary. 4. 老實說，人類沒有比動物文明。 On the contrary, animals never abandon their owners and make them become "stray owners." In a sense, 5. 人類事實上仍然必須向動物學習，不是嗎？

❷ tend to 傾向於、易於　be faced with/encounter 面臨
financial problem 財務問題　abandon 拋棄
❸ share...with 與…分享
❹ honestly speaking 老實說　be not more + Adj + than... …沒有比…
civilized 文明
❺ actually/in fact 事實上、其實

1. _____

2. _____

3. _____

4. _____

5. _____

 Sentence Combination 句子合併

說明 請根據提示，將各題的兩個句子合併成一個語意通順、語法正確的英文句子。

1. so as to

Johnny is studying in the USA.

He wants to get a Ph.D. degree.

➡ _____

2. In addition to...,

Nancy went jogging last Wednesday.

Nancy also went swimming last Wednesday.

➡ _____

3. despite

It snowed heavily outside.

The baseball game still went on.

➡ _____

4. why

The teacher asked Jennifer something.

Jennifer was late for school.

➡ _____

5. help

Mom cleaned up the house before Lunar New Year's Eve.

We helped Mom out.

➡ _____

Guided Translation 克漏式翻譯

說明 下面一段短文中，有數處以中文呈現，請利用上下文線索及提示（如單字、片語等）將其譯成正確、通順、達意且前後連貫的英文。

People usually think that entertainment costs a lot of money. 1. 聽音樂會，看電影或看球賽令人愉快的但很昂貴。 The following might help you 2. 假如你認為沒花很多錢就玩得不愉快。 First, walk out of your house and just see what other people are doing on the busy streets. With a calm mind, 3. 你對這世界會有全新的想法。 Even if you are not interested in them, 4. 新鮮的空氣和溫暖的陽光對你也有益。 Second, find a corner in the park, get a cup of coffee, and 5. 免費享受街頭藝人所演奏的音樂。 If you are lucky enough, you can also request a song without throwing any coins into their hats. Next time, if you need free entertainment, you will know what to do.

❶ concert 音樂會、演唱會　ball games 球賽　enjoyable 令人愉快的
❷ have a good time/fun 玩的愉快　without... 沒有…
❸ toward... 對於…　brand/whole new 全新的
❹ be beneficial/good to 對…有益處
❺ street entertainer 街頭藝人　for free 免費

1. _____

2. _____

3. _____

4. _____

5. _____

 Sentence Combination 句子合併

說明 請根據提示，將各題的兩個句子合併成一個語意通順、語法正確的英文句子。

1. as

David couldn't buy the ticket to the movie.

David decided to stay home watching TV.

➡ _____

2. Not until...

Bobby was seriously ill.

Bobby finally realized the importance of health.

➡ _____

3. rather than

Alan walked to school.

Alan didn't take the MRT.

➡ _____

4. thanks to

Stanley helped me in time.

I finished my history report on time.

➡ _____

5. it is...to...

To master English is difficult.

I find it difficult.

➡ _____

Guided Translation 克漏式翻譯

說明 下面一段短文中，有數處以中文呈現，請利用上下文線索及提示（如單字、片語等）將其譯成正確、通順、達意且前後連貫的英文。

To save our earth, 1. 人們可以採取許多預防的方法去對抗污染。 For example, use energy-saving devices rather than equipment which consumes a large amount of electricity or batteries. 2. 電池污染環境，而且大部分的都無法重複使用。 Next, don't throw away old toys or clothes, send them to the orphanages or the poor instead. 3. 把你不需要的送給有需要的人。 It is not wasted. In addition, 4. 你不需要水時要關掉 and take short showers instead of baths. It saves a lot of water. Last, 5. 用低能源的燈泡來省電。 It's everybody's business to protect the earth. Let's help to save it.

---

❶ take measure 採取方法　preventive 預防的
❷ reusable 可重覆使用的
❸ whoever/anyone who 任何人
❹ turn off/on 關閉/打開
❺ low-energy 低能源的

---

1. _____

2. _____

3. _____

4. _____

5. _____

Sentence Combination 句子合併

說明 請根據提示，將各題的兩個句子合併成一個語意通順、語法正確的英文句子。

1. instead of

Mom didn't go shopping last Saturday.

Mom was busy doing housework last Saturday.

 _____

2. ..., with

Adam went to his sister's wedding.

Adam's heart was filled with happiness.

 _____

3. however

The work was really difficult.

Jason still decided to give it a try.

 _____

4. the + Adj₁-er/Adv₁-er..., the + Adj₂-er/Adv₂-er...

You study more.

You will get better grades.

 _____

5. whose

Sarah is a famous opera singer.

Her albums are sold all over the world.

 _____

Guided Translation 克漏式翻譯

說明 下面一段短文中，有數處以中文呈現，請利用上下文線索及提示（如單字、片語等）將其譯成正確、通順、達意且前後連貫的英文。

Taiwanese women have had better education and job opportunities; the role of women is changing. 1. 很多女性不再視婚姻和養育孩子為理所當然。 To them, marriage and child bearing are an option but not a necessity. 2. 不像過去傳統台灣女性，現代女性在經濟上獨立。 Pursing their own interest, 3. 他們在專業成就上得到滿足感。 They pay no attention to the declining birthrate, which is a big headache to government officials. 4. 當局想盡每個方法來鼓勵女性生育小孩， but in vain. That's because Taiwanese women's thinking is changing. 5. 他們已經變成新台灣女性。

---

❶ no longer... 不再　take...for granted 視…為理所當然
　 raise (children) 養育小孩
❷ unlike 不像、不同於　economically independent 經濟獨立的
❸ find satisification in 在…得到（找到）滿足感　professional 專業的
❹ the authorities 當局　each and every 每個

---

1. _____

2. _____

3. _____

4. _____

5. _____

Sentence Combination 句子合併

說明 請根據提示，將各題的兩個句子合併成一個語意通順、語法正確的英文句子。

1. for fear of

I checked my phone book several times.

I was afraid of dialing the wrong number.

➡ _____

2. both

We sang at Mary's birthday party.

We danced at Mary's birthday party, too.

➡ _____

3. either

George may find a job.

George may go to graduate school.

➡ _____

4. forget

I didn't send Grace flowers on Valentine's Day.

I forgot that.

➡ _____

5. find + O + OC (V)

Rick cheated on the final exam.

The teacher found that.

➡ _____

Guided Translation 克漏式翻譯

說明 下面一段短文中，有數處以中文呈現，請利用上下文線索及提示（如單字、片語等）將其譯成正確、通順、達意且前後連貫的英文。

Dear George,

I, on behalf of my family, really hope that you will come and visit us in Taiwan during this coming summer vacation. 1. 雖然台灣離你美國的家很遠， and it costs a lot for you to fly here, 2. 但你將有較多的機會學習和說中文。 Besides, my family all love to have you stay here with us and 3. 我們也已經為你準備了一間房間。 Please don't worry because all of us can speak some English. We also have cable TV, 4. 其中包括一些你喜歡的電視節目。 I'll bet you will never get homesick. If you have any questions about all of this, just let me know. 5. 我們全家都期待很快在台灣和你見面。

Sincerely yours,

David Wang

❶ on behalf of 代表　far away from 遠離
❸ ....as well …也
❹ include 包括　some of... 其中一些…
❺ look forward to + V-ing 期待

1. _____

2. _____

3. _____

4. _____

5. _____

Sentence Combination 句子合併

說明 請根據提示，將各題的兩個句子合併成一個語意通順、語法正確的英文句子。

1. believe

To survive a severe earthquake is a miracle.

Most people believe it a miracle.

 _____

2. the same as

My bike is WDJ 549.

Fred's bike is WDJ 549.

 _____

3. be used to

Johnny goes jogging every Saturday morning.

Johnny is used to it.

 _____

4. should

Helen told her mother a lie.

Helen should not do it.

 _____

5. not only...but also...

Rita does well in her studies.

Rita is good at playing tennis.

 _____

Guided Translation 克漏式翻譯

說明 下面一段短文中，有數處以中文呈現，請利用上下文線索及提示（如單字、片語等）將其譯成正確、通順、達意且前後連貫的英文。

Cell phones are really one of the great technological inventions of the 20th century. 1. 手機讓人們不論在何時何地都能與任何人溝通。 Parents use cell phones to talk to their children when they get stuck in traffic. 2. 回家途中，學生們跟同學或朋友講手機 to kill boring time. Bosses use cell phones to give orders to their employees. 3. 手機真的在我們日常生活中扮演很重要的角色。 On the other hand, using cell phones has negative effects. For example, public places, such as restaurants, train stations, or even on the buses 4. 變得更吵，因為總是有人在講手機。 In addition, cell phones make people meet face to face less frequently. Somewhat 5. 人與人之間的關係被破壞只因為人們很少彼此見面。 Are the cell phones really great inventions? It depends on how you think of it.

❶ make it possible for....to V 使…變成可能　communicate with 溝通
　wherever = no matter where 無論何處、地　whenever = no matter when
❷ on one's way to 往…的途中　on the cell phone/phone 講手機/電話
❸ play a vital/an importent role in 扮演重要的角色

1. _____

2. _____

3. _____

4. _____

5. _____

Sentence Combination 句子合併

說明 請根據提示，將各題的兩個句子合併成一個語意通順、語法正確的英文句子。

1. Besides...,

Cathy can speak French fluently.

Cathy can speak English fluently.

 _____

2. pay

I bought a new bike.

The new bike cost NT$7500.

 _____

3. see

I saw Tom in the park.

He was riding a bike in the park.

 _____

4. take

I walk to school every day.

I spend 30 minutes doing it.

 _____

5. junior

Julia is 24 years old.

Nancy is 37 years old.

 _____

Guided Translation 克漏式翻譯

說明 下面一段短文中，有數處以中文呈現，請利用上下文線索及提示（如單字、片語等）將其譯成正確、通順、達意且前後連貫的英文。

Is it really appropriate for children to start learning as young as possible? 1. 雖然在台灣，孩子之間的課業競爭很激烈， yet small kids really don't need to begin learning at such an early age. 2. 大部份的孩童上補習班 after they have six or seven classes each day at school. Their parents hold the belief that 3. 小孩學越多，成績就會越好。 However, education experts believe that 4. 太多功課，玩樂不夠對孩童不好。 Children who spend too much time studying often have less time to have fun. Consequently, 5. 他們會對課業提不起興趣，甚至拒絕學習。 One piece of advice to parents—your children need time to relax and enjoy their childhood.

---

❶ competition (among/between) …(間) 的競爭　keen 激烈
❷ go to cram school 上補習班
❸ the more..., the better... 越多…越好
❹ schoolwork 課業
❺ show/take no interest in 對…沒興趣

---

1. _____

2. _____

3. _____

4. _____

5. _____

 Sentence Combination 句子合併

說明 請根據提示，將各題的兩個句子合併成一個語意通順、語法正確的英文句子。

1. spend

I spent one hour in the park.

I played Frisbee with my brother there.

➡ _____

2. as soon as

David got home yesterday afternoon.

He cooked dinner immediately.

➡ _____

3. in spite of

Sandra felt sick this morning.

She went to work as usual.

➡ _____

4. find it + Adj

I find something interesting.

Taking a walk after dinner is interesting.

➡ _____

5. prefer...to...

I like to play basketball.

I don't like to go jogging.

➡ _____

Guided Translation 克漏式翻譯

說明 下面一段短文中，有數處以中文呈現，請利用上下文線索及提示（如單字、片語等）將其譯成正確、通順、達意且前後連貫的英文。

It is said that many years ago, a Japanese doctor created the four basic personality traits, Blood Type A, B, O and AB. Blood Type A people 1. 據說較安靜有禮貌， but they always worry too much and have trouble making decisions. 2. B 型的人有創意又樂觀。 Besides, they are likely to be good cooks or animal lovers. But they forget things easily and 3. 採取行動前沒仔細思考。 Those with Blood Type O are confident and athletic. 4. 他們是好的領袖，但對人們的需求不敏感。 Blood Type AB people seem to be happy and think about things deeply. 5. 他們很酷又受歡迎，但不容易原諒別人。 In a word, blood type is just a kind of statistics for your reference; don't be superstitious about it.

❶ S + be believed/said to be 據說
❷ with... 擁有 creative 創意的 optimistic 樂觀的
❸ take action 行動
❹ be sensitive to 對…敏感
❺ popular 受歡迎的

1. _____

2. _____

3. _____

4. _____

5. _____

Sentence Combination 句子合併

說明 請根據提示，將各題的兩個句子合併成一個語意通順、語法正確的英文句子。

1. because of

Brian was very lazy.

He didn't do well in his studies.

➽ _____

2. of...

There are forty students in the class.

John runs faster than any of them.

➽ _____

3. if

I am not Andy.

I can not make the decision.

➽ _____

4. ...how...

How did he do it?

We really had no idea of it.

➽ _____

5. too...to...

Wilson was very busy.

Wilson had no time to go on a vacation with his wife.

➽ _____

■■ *Guided Translation* 克漏式翻譯

說明 下面一段短文中，有數處以中文呈現，請利用上下文線索及提示（如單字、片語等）將其譯成正確、通順、達意且前後連貫的英文。

Chinese calligraphy has long been regarded as one of the highest forms of art in China. 1. <u>傑出的書法家很受重視</u> so that their works have been high priced collection of art collectors. It is believed that 2. <u>在過去書法曾經在中國文化裡扮演重要的角色</u> though it is no longer widely practiced in China. However, 3. <u>它已經被傳到其它的亞洲國家，例如日本及韓國。</u> In Taiwan, the use of calligraphy 4. <u>可能沒像在上述國家那樣普遍。</u> It's a pity that 5. <u>現今只有少數學童偶而寫書法</u> here in Taiwan.

---

❶ excellent 傑出的　calligrapher 書法家　be highly valued 受到高度重視

❷ calligraphy 書法　play an important role in 扮演重要角色

❸ spread 流傳　such as... 例如

❹ as...as 與…一樣　popular 普遍的　above 以上的…

❺ now/nowadays 現在、現今　once in a while/from time to time/at times 偶而

---

1. _____

2. _____

3. _____

4. _____

5. _____

英文寫作測驗：句子合併&克漏式翻譯

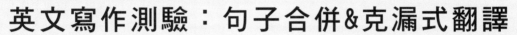

Writing Test: Sentence Combination & Guided Translation

解答解析篇

🔑 Answer Keys

1

🔹 句子合併

1. Although George has failed English tests for two times, he still does not give up.

2. I neither stayed at home nor went picnicking with my friends last Sunday.

👉 neither...nor... 後接的詞性必須一致，表示「兩者皆非」。

3. The final soccer game was postponed due to a heavy storm.

👉 due to + N，表示「原因」。

4. Nancy has been sleeping since three o'clock.

5. If I had had enough money last year, I could have bought a new car.

👉 If + S + had + V-en..., S + would/could/should/might + have + V-en 表示「與過去事實不符」。

🔹 克漏式翻譯

1. Most people feel tired once in a while.

2. A proper diet is one of the easiest ways to avoid fatigue

3. Another way to prevent fatigue is to exercise regularly.

👉 exercise regularly 規律的運動
regular exercise 為名詞片語

4. As a result/Therefore, many people <u>gain weight</u>/<u>become heavy</u>

5. Exercise, like jogging, hiking, swimming and so on,

2

🔹 句子合併

1. I was born in Fongyuan, where I spent my childhood.

👉 Fongyuan (豐原) 為一地名，故用非限定用法的關係副詞 where 連接。

2. Hillary not only rented a new apartment for her son but also bought a new car for her daughter.

👉 not only...but also 不僅⋯而且⋯ 後接的詞性須一致。

3. (1) Grace is heavier than Jean (by 20 pounds).
   (2) Grace weighs more than Jean (by 20 pounds).

👉 than 為比較級用法，by 為表示「差距」。

4. Fred didn't study hard; as a result, he flunked three subjects.

👉 as a result/therefore 因此，表示因果關係。

5. The car (which is) made in Germany was taken away by the police.

👉 關係代名詞 + be + V-en，「關係代名詞 + be」可省略。

🔹 克漏式翻譯

1. These cars are divided into two classes.

2. Business class is more comfortable, but standard one is cheaper.

3. these trains <u>make</u>/<u>produce</u> less noise and pollution than cars.

4. These stations need long platforms

5. Why not try taking a high speed train next time?

3

句子合併

1. Both Johnny and Jimmy enjoy going to the movies.

➡ both A and B 兩者都　enjoy + V-ing

2. Brian is going to tell us a touching story that happened three years ago.

➡ that 與 which 為關係代名詞用法，連接子句用以進一步修飾 a touching story。

3. Angelina arrived at the airport in time only to find that she did not have her passport with her.

➡ in time　即時

4. Jenny was one of the four people who were saved from the burning house.

➡ who 為關係代名詞，進一步說明 one of the four people 的相關資訊。

5. When Brad reaches Taipei tonight, I will invite him over for dinner.

➡ when 連接兩個句子，以現在式用以表示未來式之意。

克漏式翻譯

1. Americans think that their country is the most powerful/strongest one in the world,

2. Thousands of lives were lost

➡ hundreds/millions of 數以百計 / 百萬計

3. they were extremely shocked that they would be attacked/someone would attack them in this way.

4. They were ready to die for their beliefs,

5. Unfortunately, the terrorists have become potential enemies of the world.

4

句子合併

1. (1) As long as we never give up, we will achieve our goals.

   (2) We will achieve our goals as long as we never give up.

2. The girl with long hair is my sister.

3. (1) Bobby stayed home watching TV instead of going on swimming.

   (2) Instead of going on swimming, Bobby stayed home watching TV.

4. (1) After Johnny finished his breakfast, he hurried to school.

   (2) After finishing his breakfast, Johnny hurried to school.

➡ 使用 after/before 注意時間先後順序。若主詞相同時，after/before S + V = after/before + V-ing

5. Carlos won Helen's heart by giving her a diamond ring.

➡ win one's heart　贏得某人的心

克漏式翻譯

1. Local business, non-profit foundations and many individuals have donated more than NT$370 million dollars

2. was completely destroyed by a fire in early February, 2008.

3. promised that they would make the best use of the donations

4. he was aware that all the donors' money was hard-earned.

5. it also brought about new chances/opportunities.

5

句子合併

1. Joan should have written an English composition last Sunday.

➡ should have + V-en 過去該做而沒做
　 must have +V-en 過去肯定猜測

2. Alex read a Dear John letter from his girlfriend with tears rolling down his face.

3. Nobody knows what Jimmy wants.

➡ 表示間接問句：S₁ + V₁ + wh- 疑問詞 + S₂ + V₂....

4. I prefer Italian food to fast food.

➡ prefer V-ing/N to V-ing/N 較喜歡…而不…

5. Melky didn't concentrate in class, and nor did Steve.

➡ nor + Be/Aux + S

克漏式翻譯

1. (1) It is believed that global warming is inevitable, and humans are to blame.
　 (2) Global warming is believed to be inevitable, and humans are to blame.

2. It is very likely that global warming is caused by man-made greenhouse gas emissions.

3. Obviously, there is a strong link between public health and climate change.

4. Therefore, global warming not only threatens human life, but also makes some species extinct.

5. Please save/conserve energy and reduce/cut (down on) carbon dioxide emissions.

6

句子合併

1. As soon as I walked out of the house, I witnessed a car accident.

2. Miss Lin is such a famous fashion model that everybody knows her.

➡ such a...that 如此…以至於

3. Anna neither went shopping nor saw the movie yesterday afternoon.

➡ neither...nor... 既不是…也不是，後接的詞性必須一致，表示「兩者皆非」。

4. Jimmy got up at 6:00 this morning for fear of missing the first bus.

➡ for fear of + V-ing 以免…

5. (1) It took me three hours to search for some information on the Internet.
　 (2) I took three hours to search for some information on the Internet.

克漏式翻譯

1. Due to the global economic recession, a great number of companies are laying off their employees.

2. their children are forced to drop out of college and work part-time to help support the family.

3. Many factories are closed down and many companies go bankrupt.

4. this economic condition is three times worse than we have imagined,

➡ S + be + 數詞 + Adj-er + than....

5. we should still hold an optimistic attitude toward life.

7

📑 句子合併

1. Macy's father weighs/is three times heavier than Macy.

2. (1) John has the same cell phone as Mary (did).

    (2) Mary has the same cell phone as John (did).

➡ the same as 與…一樣

3. Ann takes a walk in the park twice a week and so does Sue.

➡ so + be/Aux + S (肯定倒裝)

    take a walk/go for a walk 散步

4. The bag (which) I am carrying is very heavy.

➡ which 為關係代名詞

5. If Julia were good at math, she could help me solve the math problem.

➡ If + S+ were/V-ed…, S + would/could/ should/might + V 表示「與現在事實不符」

📑 克漏式翻譯

1. But please stay/remain/keep calm; don't get mad/angry easily.

2. (1) They may be in a bad mood

    (2) They may not be in a good mood

3. It doesn't necessarily mean (that) they don't like you or they want to pick on you.

4. Try to think for your friends and you will feel better.

5. Isn't that what friends are for?

➡ what + Aux/be + S + for… 代表著…？

    此為附加問句，主動詞需要倒裝。

8

📑 句子合併

1. We all heard Jenny playing the piano in the next room.

2. I have no idea where she is going.

➡ Wh- 疑問詞 + S + V… (間接問句)

3. The black luggage weighs as much as the red one.

➡ as…as 和…一樣；同樣為 luggage，故後者省略以代名詞 one 代替。

4. I forgot to wake up my brother at seven o'clock this morning.

➡ forget to V 忘了要去做

    wake up sb. 叫醒某人

5. David is too busy to take his children to school every day.

➡ too Adj/Adv to V 太…而不能

📑 克漏式翻譯

1. A lot of/Lost of/Many people dream of getting/becoming rich overnight,

2. According to/Based on surveys, those who hit the jackpot tend to want it all/everything

3. most of them end up with having nothing.

4. and have to turn to professional counselors for help.

5. they would/will also become/be back to what they used to be overnight.

9

句子合併

1. Doing the housework all day made Grace very tired.
2. (1) Johnny finished the final report by himself without Jane's help.
   (2) Without Jane's help, Johnny finished the final report by himself.
3. A great number of high school students study very hard in order that they can/in order to enter their ideal universities.
4. Jenny didn't show up at the party until everyone was about to leave.
5. My father sat on the sofa, watching the evening news.
   ➭ 此為對等子句簡化的分詞構句用法。=My father sat on the sofa and watched the evering news.

克漏式翻譯

1. Today we have up to one hundred channels for us to choose from, including cable and satellite channels.
2. we keep on switching the channels and we have trouble/difficulty deciding what to watch.
3. Although TV plays an important role in our daily lives.
4. It provides breaking news about important events and widens our horizons.
   ➭ experience 經驗　vision 遠見
5. television may lead to more and more crime and violence

10

句子合併

1. Wendy is so smart that she always gets good grades in math.
   ➭ so Adj/Adv that
2. (1) As soon as Robert got home, he turned on the TV.
   (2) Robert turned on the TV as soon as he got home.
   ➭ immediately = as soon as
3. Angelina did not keep a pet at home, and neither did Sandra.
4. Marlin spends as much time as Jennifer surfing the Net every day.
5. Being late for school frequently, Edward was often punished by his homeroom teacher.
   ➭ Edward 與 He 為同一人，故省略主詞以簡化的分詞構句來表示。V_1-ing..., S + V_2...

克漏式翻譯

1. The more good listeners hear, the more sensitive they will be to what's going on around them.
2. Therefore, they have fewer enemies than others and they may become the most loved people.
3. some governmental officials are excellent listeners, but they are not popular with people.
4. they simply/only/merely listen without action.
5. Actions speak louder than words.

11

句子合併

1. Daniel is such an energetic person that he can play sports all day without taking a break.
2. The little boy is looking at the chocolate with his mouth watering.
3. There are 20 students waiting for the bus at the bus stop.
4. I would rather stay home than go out shopping on Sundays.
   ➡ would rather + V...than + V/prefer to V... rather than.../would V rather than V 寧願…而不
5. Feeling tired this morning, David fell asleep in class.

克漏式翻譯

1. is an international hunger-fighting program
2. so that they can get a clear understanding of what hunger is like.
3. It enables people to fight against world hunger and poverty
4. I wondered what on earth/in the world he was talking about,
5. I realize that we can stop world hunger if we take actions now
   ➡ 此句使用的 if 為一般直說法的條件句,用於陳述事實或表示未來可能發生的事,不是假設話氣,也沒有與事實相反。

12

句子合併

1. An old man sat on the bench in the park with his eyes closed.
   ➡ with + O + OC (V-en/V-ing)
2. Jane got up early in the morning lest she should be late for school.
3. Brad married a 25-year-old beautiful girl, whose father is a history professor at Harvard University.
4. My father has seen *Cape No.7* four times, and so has Tom's father.
5. Upon hearing the funny joke, Allen burst into laughter right away.

克漏式翻譯

1. The busy lifestyles in big cities are damaging people's spirits.
2. Even though they are surrounded by hundreds of people every day, they still feel lonely.
3. However, those who do move to the country need to make adjustments to their lifestyles and attitudes.
4. they find it hard to have the convenience that is taken for granted in big cities.
5. Unfortunately, some people can't stand leading such a country life and decide to move back to big cities again.

13

句子合併

1. Andy neither concentrated in class nor did well in extracurricular activities.
2. Despite his doctor's warning, Fred still did not quit smoking.
3. The heavy snow led to the power failure last night.
4. (1) After eating/she ate breakfast at 6:00, Gina went to school by bike.
   (2) Gina went to school by bike after eating/she ate breakfast at 6:00.
5. Only when people lose their health do they realize the importance of it.
   ➡ People realize the importance of health only when they lose it.

克漏式翻譯

1. In fact, some of them just take interest in gossip of the celebrities, such as singers, movie stars, or politicians.
2. to what extent can a reporter/journalist be trusted?
3. To satisfy readers, reporter/journalists report/cover/write embarrassing events/stories, such as love affairs and sex scandals of celebrities,
4. Who knows where the boundaries between journalism ethics and freedom of speech are?
5. they will end up with nothing and no one will believe them anymore.

14

句子合併

1. The book in which I took great interest was about gardening.
2. Brian was sitting on the sofa with his eyes wide open.
3. (1) While John is mopping the floor, his wife is busy cooking in the kitchen.
   (2) While John's wife is busy cooking in the kitchen, he is mopping the floor.
4. (1) Allen is one of my good friends.
   (2) I have many good friends, one of whom is Allen.
5. My grandpa is too old to walk fast.

克漏式翻譯

1. and explained which behaviors were not acceptable.
2. Each culture has its own taboos, customs, and rules
3. respect each culture and treat it equally.
4. Politics, religion, and sex may also be taboo subjects in other cultures.
5. (1) you don't feel like talking to them if you keep silent too long.
   (2) you wouldn't like to talk to them if you keep silent too long.

15

句子合併

1. I wonder if Steve will arrive on time.

2. George's mother always makes him wash dishes for her.

3. (1) When Fred got promoted in June, his wife was laid off.

   (2) When Fred's wife was laid off in June, he got promoled.

4. I saw Grace watching TV in the next room.

5. I have been used to eating night snacks before going to bed.

克漏式翻譯

1. one out of every four people in the world is overweight.

2. More and more people work long hours far from home every day.

3. So we get overweight easily due to the lack of exercise.

4. we are too busy to prepare a healthy meal so we grab some fast food for dinner.

5. we eat as many vegetables and fruits as possible and get enough rest and exercise.

16

句子合併

1. David's father makes a lot of money by selling fruit at the roadside.

➡ by 藉由，roadside 路邊

2. Peter left the room without saying a word.

3. Liz has lived in the United States since three years ago.

4. (1) Cindy fell asleep in the study while Jenny was doing her homework.

   (2) While Jenny was doing her homework, Cindy fell asleep in the study.

5. It is difficult for Andy to find a job.

克漏式翻譯

1. we should learn to get along with fever although it makes us uncomfortable.

2. our normal body temperature should be near 37°C (degrees Celsius).

3. In short, we think of fever as an illness.

4. Fever is usually the signal/warning of certain kind of sickness.

5. take a warm bath and drink enough water first.

17

⬛ 句子合併

1. The firefighters arrived and put out the fire.
2. The hotel where we stayed last night was near the MRT station.
3. Get up early, or you will be late for school.

➡ or 否則、不然

4. You always have to look both ways before you cross the road.
5. Linda is hungry but she does not have anything to eat.

⬛ 克漏式翻譯

1. parents and teachers are concerned that playing video games will do them harm.
2. playing video games is just a waste of time and it has nothing to do with bad behavior.
3. As long as parents can limit the amount of time their children spend playing video games,
4. some experts indicate that playing video games can be as helpful as playing sports.
5. The most important of all is / lies in moderation.

18

⬛ 句子合併

1. My mom went out without locking the door yesterday morning.
2. My brother is good at telling ghost stories to me.

➡ tell sb. a story = tell a story to sb.

3. John went to the supermarket by bicycle.
4. Colin is making faces at Lucy behind her.
5. I have no idea of what his real name is.

➡ 此為附加問句用法，主動詞需倒裝：$S_1 + V_1$ wh- $+ S_2 + V_2$

⬛ 克漏式翻譯

1. (1) The following are reasons that lead to accidents.

   (2) The following are reasons that result in accidents.

2. They are absent-minded and run the red light.
3. road users do not pay attention to road signs or (do not) obey traffic rules.
4. certain accidents happened/occurred because of drunken driving.
5. we believe that safety is everybody's business.

19

句子合併

1. He has worked on the computer for four hours.

☞ have/has + V-en + for + 一段時間

現在完成式用法

2. (1) My wife and I didn't go to the party because we were not invited by Sally.

(2) My wife and I didn't go to the party because Sally didn't invite us.

3. Mark didn't study hard for the entrance exam, so he didn't pass it.

4. Wilson never hit the jackpot, (and) nor did I.

☞ ..., nor + V + S 倒裝用法

5. I am wondering if my sister wants to go to the cinema tonight.

☞ wonder + if / whether + S + V

克漏式翻譯

1. even in rich countries, there are many homeless people.

2. (1) are out of job and can't afford their rent.

(2) have become jobless and can't afford their rent.

3. Some are those who are mentally ill and have no one to take care of/look after them.

4. may just have had a serious disagreement with their parents and have left home.

5. charities and churches provide makeshift/temporary shelters and food for the homeless,

20

句子合併

1. Barbara has been sick since yesterday morning.

☞ have/has + V-en + since + 過去時間

現在完成式用法。

2. Roger neither stole his Dad's money nor broke into his neighbor's house.

3. I don't know who lives in the next house.

☞ 間接問句用法：S_1 + V_1 + ... + wh- 疑問詞 + S_2 + V_2

4. (1) It took me one hour to walk to the main station.

(2) I took one hour to walk to the main station.

5. (1) The bridge was not closed by the authorities although a severe typhoon came.

(2) The authorities did not close the bridge although a severe typhoon came.

克漏式翻譯

1. Some people look down when they are in trouble.

2. Others still look happy and hold an optimistic attitude

3. because they always bring happiness to others.

4. (1) It's hard for us to observe anything different from their facial expressions.

(2) We hardly observe anything different from their facial expressions.

5. people experience hard times at one time or another/once in a while.

21

句子合併

1. Paul likes to read at home instead of going to the movies.

2. Powell has seven digital cameras, one of which is made in Germany

➡ and one of them 連接詞和代名詞由關係代名詞 which 代替，故改成 one of which。

3. Donna studies hard day and night lest she should fail the exam.

➡ lest...should 以免

4. Miss Lin is such a beautiful lady that a lot of handsome young men want to be her boyfriends.

5. If Diana were John, she could imagine how miserable John's life was.

➡ ❶ If + S₁ + V₁-ed/were...., S₂ + Aux + V₂.... 與現在事實相反的假設語氣用法。
  ❷ wh- + Adj + S + V，為附加問句用法，主動詞倒裝。

克漏式翻譯

1. At this time of the year, traditional markets are filled with the crowd/crowded with people.

2. they will have a big feast on Lunar New Year's Eve for family reunion.

3. hoping to bring good luck to them for the following/next year.

4. adults usually go visiting their relatives or friends and children enjoy setting off firecrackers,

5. everyone has at least a seven-day holiday,

22

句子合併

1. Angelina is not only beautiful but also attractive.

➡ not only...but also 不僅…而且

2. Harry, whose attention is never disracted, always listens carefully in class.

➡ whose 在此當所有格用。

3. People make resolutions on January 1ˢᵗ on the lunar calendar when the Chinese New Year begins.

4. If you study harder, you can do better in the entrance exam.

➡ 此句為純條件句。

5. If Morris had been innocent, he would not have been put in prison for 3 years.

➡ If + S + had + V-en..., S + would/might/should/could + have + V-en.... 此為與過去事實相反的假設語氣用法。

克漏式翻譯

1. It suddenly snows heavily in some places, where it never snows at all.

➡ where 為關係代名詞，用以附加說明 places。

2. Although leaders from all around the world regularly meet to discuss the serious issue,

3. one of the solutions is to cut greenhouse gas emissions.

4. The environmental protection policy would certainly cause the losses of some factories' profits,

5. turn out to be aimless speeches and debates.

23

⬛ 句子合併

1. You can't catch the first bus unless you get up early.

2. The soccer game was postponed as a result of heavy snow.

➦ as a result of/owing to/due to/because of 由於

3. Amanda is tall and charming, and so is Sandy.

➦ so + V + S 倒裝用法

4. I saw as many movies as Stanley did last month.

5. I borrowed four books which I was interested in from the library.

➦ which 為關係代名詞

⬛ 克漏式翻譯

1. there are often reports of people getting drowned around the island.

2. but in the rivers where people are not supposed to swim.

➦ where 為關係代名詞，用以進一步修飾說明 rivers。

3. ending up with their heads crashing onto the rocks under the water and losing their lives.

4. it is suggested/someone suggested that the police should reinforce patrols and put up more warning signs.

5. One of the effective ways is that the government should build more swimming pools

24

⬛ 句子合併

1. My father gets up early in the morning in order to take me to school.

➦ in order to/so as to 為了

2. Nick walked too slowly to catch up with us.

➦ too...to 太…而不能

3. (1) Upon getting home in the evening, Justin turned on the TV.

   (2) Justin turned on the TV upon getting home in the evening.

➦ upon + V-ing/as soon as S + V 一…就

4. Megan is senior to Wilson (by 9 years).

➦ be senior/junior to 比…年長/年輕

   Wilson is junior to Megan (by 9 years).

5. The book cost me NT$200.

➦ S + cost + sb + 金錢

⬛ 克漏式翻譯

1. Its economic condition once was the pride of the Taiwanese people

2. Taiwan is gradually becoming a so-called "M-shaped" society

3. That is, the rich become richer and the poor become poorer.

4. What's worse, the unemployment rate is increasing

5. It's really a problem that our government should take seriously.

25

句子合併

1. My mom went to the supermarket, where she did the shopping.

▶ where 為關係代名詞，用以進一步修飾說明 supermarket。

2. (1) I say good night to my parents before I go to bed.

   (2) Before I go to bed, I say good night to my parents.

3. Raymond's father makes him wash his car twice a week.

▶ make + O + Adj/V

4. In spite of much opposition, the government is still planning to build another nuclear plant.

▶ despite/in spite of + N 儘管/雖然

5. To my surprise, Jenny got first place in the English speech contest.

▶ to one's surprise 令人驚奇的是…

克漏式翻譯

1. More and more schoolchildren are overweight

2. because obesity may result in/lead to some diseases in the future,

3. Owing to too much schoolwork and frequent test, they hardly have time to take exercise.

4. including French fries, soda drinks and hamburgers which contain a lot of calories.

5. parents prepare healthy food for their children each and every meal.

26

句子合併

1. As soon as Joseph heard the news of his father's death, he burst into tears.

▶ burst into + N

   burst out + V-ing 突然…

2. It snowed heavily outside; nevertheless, Peter went camping as usual.

▶ however/nevertheless/nonetheless 然而

   as usual 一如往常

3. (1) Jack played golf last weekend, and so did Scott.

   (2) Scott played golf last weekend, and so did Jack.

4. Roger prefers reading novels to surfing the Net.

▶ prefer + V-ing/N + to + V-ing/N 喜歡…勝過於…

5. If the weather is fine tomorrow, we will go picnicking tomorrow.

克漏式翻譯

1. teenager listen to music on their MP3 players while going for a walk, taking the MRT or studying for tests.

2. listening to music on the MP3 player for long hours may cause great damage to hearing.

3. Gradually, they are used to the noise,

4. Therefore, turn down the MP3 player next time you listen to it.

5. take good care of your ears right now.

27

▪ 句子合併

1. Mandy would rather watch TV at home than go to the library.

   ▶ would rather...than.... 寧願…而不願

2. He went to Tainan by bus yesterday.

   ▶ by + 交通工具　搭乘…

3. I got a letter which was written in English.

4. Cathy is both charming and beautiful.

5. Craig not only cooked dinner but also washed clothes yesterday evening.

▪ 克漏式翻譯

1. they either don't have time for it or do not get into the habit of eating breakfast.

2. (1) nearly 40 percent of people go to work or school without eating breakfast.

   (2) nearly 40 percent of people don't eat breakfast before going to work or school.

3. On the contrary, those who do not eat breakfast easily gain weight.

4. those/people who eat/have breakfast have better academic performance than those who don't.

5. eating/having enough breakfast enables one to think more logically and have better memory.

28

▪ 句子合併

1. Would you please tell me where the bus station is?

   ▶ 間接問句用法：wh- 疑問詞 + S + V

2. Wendy goes jogging every morning in order to lose weight.

   ▶ in order to/so as to

3. Despite his hard work, Wilson failed the exam.

   ▶ despite/in spite of N　儘管

4. You had better work on your report soon; otherwise, you will not meet the deadline.

   ▶ work on　致力於

   　meet the deadline　按時完成

5. Roger didn't realize the importance of health until he had a heart attack.

   ▶ heart attack　心臟病

▪ 克漏式翻譯

1. sending sky lanterns into the sky is not only a popular folklore activity

2. Legend has it that in the past robbers often invaded the villages,

3. They would rob villagers of their belongings away, and the village is left empty.

4. the village heads would launch sky lanterns, telling villagers

   ▶ S₁ + V₁..., V₂-ing.... 分詞構句用法

5. which conveys wishes to Gods or represents peace.

29

🔹 句子合併

1. A mountaineer named Fred Johnson got lost in the mountains last week.

   ➡ 省略 who is named Fred Johnson... 的 who is。mountaineer 登山客

2. Follow the doctor's advice, or your won't get healthy.

   ➡ or 為連接詞，表示「否則」。

   take/follow one's advice 遵照…建議

3. The harder you study, the better grades you may get.

4. There are 20 students waiting for the bus at the bus stop.

   ➡ there + be + N/V-ing

5. Andy studies Russia four hours a day so that he can study in Russia some day.

   ➡ so/in order + that-clause

🔹 克漏式翻譯

1. (1) It seems that they are in good condition

   (2) They seem to be in good condition

2. tens of thousands of people were waiting in line to watch these two lovely animals.

   ➡ It seems that + S + V...

   =S + seem to + V...

3. they enjoy the bamboo feasts in the year-round air-conditioned environment.

4. make other animals in the zoo jealous.

5. because we have never seen so many people in the zoo (at this time of the year) for such a long time.

30

🔹 句子合併

1. Chien-ming Wang is such a wonderful pitcher that he has a lot of fans in Taiwan.

2. I don't have any idea at all what Lucy's address is.

3. Succeeding in the college entrance exam, Bob decided to have a study tour in the US.

   ➡ 分詞構句用法，前後主詞一致，將前面主詞去掉，動詞改為 V-ing。

4. Neither Alice nor Nick watched the soap opera last night.

5. (1) Apologize to David; otherwise, you will be punished by your homeroom teacher.

   (2) You should apologize to David; otherwise, you will be punished by your homeroom teacher.

   ➡ 此句也可用 if 改寫成 If you don't apologize to David, you will be punished by your homeroom teacher.

🔹 克漏式翻譯

1. When I come home from school, there is no one at home.

2. It's more fun to check my e-mail from them than to get/receive their phone calls.

3. through/by e-mail I am able to keep/stay in touch with my friends who live far away/in the distance.

   ➡ lose touch with 與…失去聯絡

4. nor wait for (a couple of) days for my friends to write back.

5. It saves both time and money.

31

句子合併

1. It started to rain while we were playing basketball.

2. My brother works hard so that he may make more money.

➭ so/in order + that-clause

3. Those who often exercise regularly are healthy.

➭ those/people who 凡是⋯的人

4. The National Palace Museum, which is one of the must-go spots in Taipei, attracts a lot of foreign tourists.

➭ must-go 必到、必遊的

5. (1) Besides writing stories, Nancy enjoys making movies.

   (2) Besides making movies, Nancy enjoys writing stories.

➭ besides + V-ing 除了⋯之外還

克漏式翻譯

1. There are more and more overweight children nowadays.

2. few children do not eat snacks while they are watching TV.

3. What's worse, these junk foods are rich in/ contain a lot of fat, sugar, and salt,

4. The more TV children watch, the heavier they get.

5. cut down on/reduce the time they watch TV and have snacks.

32

句子合併

1. I love to talk to Dr. Lin, who is very kind and knowledgeable.

2. Morris is so lucky that he has hit the jackpot two times.

➭ so + Adj...that... 如此⋯以至於

3. Not only do local people enjoy sending sky lanterns into the sky, but also visitors admire the wonderful celebration.

4. Seeing her parents at the airport, Angela cried and ran to them.

➭ V_1-ing..., S + V_2..., 省略相同主詞的分詞構句用法

5. The green backpack is inferior to the black one.

➭ be + inferior/superior + to 比⋯劣/優

The black backpack is superior to the green one.

克漏式翻譯

1. are humans really pets' best friends?

2. (1) people tend to abandon their pets when they are faced with financial problems.

   (2) when people encounter financial problems, they tend to abandon their pets.

3. Pets share happiness and sorrow with their owners,

4. Honestly speaking, humans are not more civilized than animals.

5. human beings actually still need to learn from animals, don't they?

➭ S + V/be..., doesn't/don't/isn't/aren't + S? 附加問句用法。

33

句子合併

1. Johnny is studying in the USA so as to get a Ph.D. degree.

➡ so as to/in order to + V 為了

2. In addition to going jogging last Wednesday, Nancy went swimming.

➡ in addition to/on top of/besides + V-ing/N 除了…之外還

3. (1) Despite the heavy snow outside, the baseball game went on.

   (2) The baseball game went on despite the heavy snow outside.

➡ despite/in spite of + N 儘管；雖然

4. The teacher asked Jennifer why she was late for school.

➡ 間接問句用法：S_1 + V_1 + … wh- 疑問詞 + S_2 + V_2

5. We helped Mom clean up the house before Lunar New Year's Eve.

克漏式翻譯

1. Concerts, movies, and ball games are enjoyable but expensive.

2. if you think you won't have a good time without spending much money.

3. you will have a brand/whole new thinking toward the world.

4. the fresh air and warm sunshine are beneficial/good to you.

5. (1) enjoy the music played by street entertainers for free.

   (2) enjoy street entertainers' performance for free.

34

句子合併

1. As David couldn't buy the ticket to the movie, he decided to stay home watching TV.

2. Not until Bobby was seriously ill did he finally realize the importance of health.

➡ Not until + S_1 + V_1…Aux + S_2 + V_2…. 否定詞置於句首時，須採部分倒裝。

3. Alan walked to school rather than took the MRT.

➡ rather than 而不是

4. Thanks to Stanley's timely help, I finished my history report on time.

➡ thanks to + N 幸虧　timely 即時的

5. It is difficult for me to master English.

➡ S + find/think/make it + Adj + to + V

I find it difficult to master English.

克漏式翻譯

1. people can take many preventive measures to fight/combat pollution.

2. Batteries pollute the environment, and most of them are not reusable.

3. Give what you don't need anymore to whoever/anyone who needs it.

4. (1) turn the water off when you don't need it

   (2) turn off the water when you don't need it

5. (1) save electricity by using low-energy light bulbs.

   (2) use low-energy light bulbs to save electricity.

35

▐ 句子合併

1. Mom was busy doing housework instead of going shopping last Saturday.

▐➔ instead of + V-ing

be busy + V-ing 忙於

2. Adam went to his sister's wedding, with his heart filled with happiness.

▐➔ ...with + O + OC (V-ing/V-en) 帶著…

3. The work was really difficult; however, he still decided to give it a try.

4. The more you study, the better grades you will get.

5. Sarah is a famous opera singer, whose albums are sold all over the world.

▐ 克漏式翻譯

1. Many women no longer take marriage and child-raising for granted.

2. Unlike traditional Taiwanese women in the past, modern women are economically independent.

3. they find satisfaction in their professional achievement.

4. The authorities try each and every way to encourage women to have children,

5. They have already become new Taiwanese women.

36

▐ 句子合併

1. I checked my phone book several times for fear of dialing the wrong number.

▐➔ for fear of 以免

2. We both sang and danced at Mary's birthday party.

3. George may either find a job or go to graduate school.

▐➔ either...or... 不是…就是…

graduate school 研究所

4. (1) I forgot to send Grace flowers on Valentine's Day.

(2) I forgot that I didn't send Grace flowers on Valentine's Day.

▐➔ forget + to V 忘了去做

forget + V-ing 忘了做過

5. The teacher found Rick cheating on/at the final exam.

▐ 克漏式翻譯

1. Although Taiwan is quite far away from your home in America,

2. (yet) you will have more chances to learn and speak Chinese.

3. we have already prepared a room for you as well.

4. (1) which includes some of your favorite TV programs.

(2) including some of your favorite TV programs.

5. All my family are looking forward to seeing you soon here in Taiwan.

37

📑 句子合併

1. Most people believe it a miracle to survive a severe earthquake.
2. My bike is the same as Fred's.
3. Johnny is used to going jogging every Saturday morning.

▶ be used to V-ing/N 習慣、適應

4. Helen should not have told her mother a lie.
5. Rita not only does well in her studies but also is good at playing tennis.

📑 克漏式翻譯

1. Cell phones make it possible for people to communicate with anyone whenever and wherever they are.
2. On their way home, students talk to their classmates or friends on the cell phones
3. Cell phones really play <u>a vital</u>/<u>an important</u> role in our everyday life.
4. are becoming noisier because there are always some people (talking) on the cell phones.
5. relations among people are damaged just because people seldom see each other.

38

📑 句子合併

1. Besides (speaking) French, Cathy can speak English fluently.
2. I paid NT$7500 for the new bike.

▶ pay + 人 + 錢 for 物

3. I saw Tom riding a bike in the park.

▶ see/watch/look at/hear/listen to/feel + O + V-ing/V 感官動詞的用法

4. It takes me 30 minutes to walk to school every day.

▶ it takes sb + 時間 + to + V

5. Julia is junior to Nancy (by 7 years).

▶ be junior/senior to 比…年輕/年長

Nancy is senior to Julia (by 7 years).

📑 克漏式翻譯

1. Although academic competition among kids in Taiwan is very keen,
2. Most of the schoolchildren go to cram school
3. the more their children learn, the better grades they will get.
4. too much schoolwork and not enough entertainment is bad for schoolchildren.
5. they will show/take no interest in their studies and even refuse to learn.

39

⬛ 句子合併

1. I spent one hour playing Frisbee with my brother in the park.

➡ spend + 時間 + V-ing

2. (1) As soon as David got home yesterday afternoon, he cooked dinner.

   (2) David cooked dinner as soon as he got home yesterday afternoon.

➡ as soon as = immediately 一…就

3. (1) In spite of feeling sick this morning, Sandra went to work as usual.

   (2) In spite of the fact that Sandra felt sick this morning, she went to work as usual.

➡ in spite of V-ing/N = in spite of the fact that /although 儘管

4. I find it interesting to take a walk after dinner.

➡ find + O + OC (Adj) + to V

5. I prefer playing basketball to going jogging.

➡ prefer + V-ing/N + to + V-ing/N
   較喜歡…而不喜歡

⬛ 克漏式翻譯

1. are believed/said to be quiet and polite,

2. People with Blood Type B are creative and optimistic.

3. don't think well before they take actions.

4. They are good leaders but not sensitive to people's needs.

5. They are cool and popular but they don't easily forgive others.

40

⬛ 句子合併

1. Brain didn't do well in his studies because of his laziness.

➡ because of/owing to/due to/as a result of
   因為；由於

2. (1) Of all the forty students in the class, John runs the fastest.

   (2) John runs the fastest of all the forty students in the class.

3. If I were Andy, I could make the decision.

4. We really had no idea how he did it.

5. Wilson was too busy to go on a vacation with his wife.

➡ too + adj./adv + to + V 太…而不

⬛ 克漏式翻譯

1. Excellent calligraphers were highly valued

2. in the past calligraphy once played an important role in Chinese culture

3. it has been spread to other Asian countries, such as Japan and Korea.

4. might not be as popular as it is in the above countries.

5. nowadays/now only a few schoolchildren practice calligraphy once in a while

1200 Words for CEE 精選 1200 單字書

單字書編排理念的最大突破！使用方式徹底革新！

◎ 從大考試題文章段落中精選 1200 個單字，平均分配為 48 週、每週 5 天、每天 5 個單字的學習份量。每天固定累積單字量，一年之後絕對大有斬獲！

◎ 特別強調從上下文去了解單字及其用法，除了幫助吸收與記憶，還可增進閱讀能力，一舉兩得！

◎ 字彙題的編撰著重於提供足夠的作答線索，凸顯單字的意思與使用情境。

◎ 另外從段落中擷取重要慣用語或搭配用字，在學習單字之餘，也可以順便加強片語實力。

英文讀寫萬試通

◎ 本書由車畇庭審定，三民英語編輯小組彙編。

◎ 適用於學測、指考、全民英檢初、中級。

◎ 全書共 16 回，前 3 回分別解說初、中、高階閱讀技巧，後 13 回仿大考閱測題型。

◎ 附解析本，含文章翻譯、完整答題思路與答題模板。

◎ 學校團體訂購附 3 回贈卷，供教師即時驗收學生的學習成效。

大考翻譯實戰題本（全新改版）

◎ 全新編排五大主題架構，串聯三十回三百句練習，爆量刷題練手感。

◎ 融入時事及新課綱議題，取材多元豐富又生活化，命題趨勢一把抓。

◎ 彙整大考熱門翻譯句型，提供建議寫法參考字詞，循序漸進好容易。

◎ 解析本收錄單字補充包，有效擴增翻譯寫作用字，翻譯技能點到滿。

20分鐘稱霸大考英文作文

第一本專為大考考生所設計的英文作文練習本！

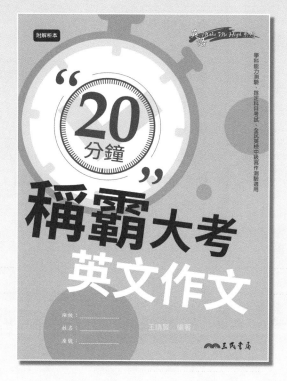

王靖賢　編著

◆ 共 16 回作文練習，涵蓋大考作文三大題型：看圖寫作、主題寫作、信函寫作。

◆ 根據近年學測及指考趨勢精心出題，題型多元且擬真度高。

◆ 每回作文練習皆有為考生精選的英文名言雋語，增強考生備考戰力。

◆ 附解析本，方便攜帶。針對每回作文題目提供寫作架構圖，讓寫作脈絡一目了然，並提供範文、寫作要點、寫作撇步及好用詞彙，讓你一本在手，即可隨時增強英文作文能力。

基礎英文法養成篇

英文學很久，文法還是囧？
本書助你釐清「觀念」、抓對「重點」、舉一反三「練習」，
不用砍掉重練，也能無縫接軌、輕鬆養成英文法！

陳曉菁　編著

◆ 每章節精選普高技高必備文法重點，編排循序
　漸進。

◆ 以圖表統整文法觀念與例句，視覺化學習組織
　概念。

◆ 將時態比喻為「河流」，假設語氣比喻為「時
　光機」，顛覆枯燥文法印象。

◆ 「文法小精靈」適時補充說明，「文法傳送門」
　提供相關文法知識章節，學習更全面。

◆ 依據文法重點設計多元題型，透過練習釐清觀
　念，融會貫通熟練文法。